General Editor:	David Jollands
Design Director:	Elwyn Blacker
Consultant Authors:	Roy Edwards
	Alan Hibbert
	Jim Hudson
	John Little
	John Mason
	Cleland McVeigh
	Peter Metcalfe
	Beverley Moody
	Patrick Moore
	Keith Porter
	Tim Pridgeon
	Derek Slack
	Ian Soden
	Tony Soper
	Alan Thomas
Research Editor:	Simon Jollands
Design and Production:	BLA Publishing Limited
	Michael Blacker
	Simon Blacker
	Margaret Hickey
	Graeme Little
	Alison Lawrenson
Artists:	Paul Doherty
	Hayward & Martin
	Dennis Knight
	Richard Lewis
	Steve Lings/Linden Artists
	Eric Thomas
	Rosie Vane-Wright

CAMBRIDGE SCIENCE UNIVERSE

LANGUAGE AND COMMUNICATION

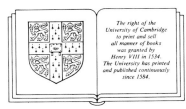

The right of the
University of Cambridge
to print and sell
all manner of books
was granted by
Henry VIII in 1534.
The University has printed
and published continuously
since 1584.

CAMBRIDGE UNIVERSITY PRESS

Cambridge · London · New York · New Rochelle · Melbourne · Sydney

Acknowledgements

The publishers wish to thank the following organizations for their invaluable assistance in the preparation of this book.

British Telecom
Canon (UK)
Central Electricity Generating Board
Ford Motor Company
Kodak Museum
NASA
National Film Board of Canada
Philips International
Royal Greenwich Observatory
Royal Smeets Offset
Shell
Sony (UK)
Southern Positives and Negatives (SPAN)
Standard Telephones and Cables
United Nations Organization
US Information Service

Published by the Press Syndicate of
the University of Cambridge,
The Pitt Building, Trumpington Street,
Cambridge CB2 1RP
32 East 57th Street, New York, NY 10022, USA
296 Beaconsfield Parade, Middle Park,
Melbourne 3206, Australia

© BLA Publishing Limited 1984

First published 1984

Library of Congress Catalog Card Number: 83-25253

British Library Cataloguing in Publication Data

Cambridge science universe.
Vol. 2: Language and communication
1. Science — Juvenile Literature
I. Jollands, David
500   Q163

ISBN 0-521-25998-3

This book was designed and produced by
BLA Publishing Limited, The Studio,
Newchapel Road, Lingfield, Surrey, England.

Also in LONDON · HONG KONG · TAIPEI · NEW YORK · SINGAPORE
A Ling Kee Company

Phototypeset in Great Britain by
Southern Positives and Negatives (SPAN).
Colour origination by Chris Willcock Reproductions
and Premier Graphics.
Printed and bound in The Netherlands by
Royal Smeets Offset BV, Weert.

Photographic credits

t = top   b = bottom   l = left   r = right   c = centre

Cover photographs: *tl* Stephen Dalton/NHPA; *tc* Douglas Dickins/NHPA; *tr* ZEFA; *bl* ZEFA/NASA; *br* Barry Lewis/Observer Picture Library.

Title page: United Nations

4 Barry Lewis/Observer Picture Library; 5*t*, 5*b*, 5*l*, 6*r* ZEFA; 7*l* Douglas Dickins/NHPA; 7*tr* Stephen Dalton/NHPA; 12 ZEFA; 14 Michael Holford; 15, 16 Michael Holford/British Museum; 18 Michael Holford; 19*tl* Mary Evans Picture Library; 19*tr* Mansell Collection; 19*bl* The National Gallery, London; 19*br* Mansell Collection; 20 ZEFA; 21*l* Paul Brierley; 21*r* ZEFA; 22*t* Royal Smeets Offset; 22*b* Paul Brierley; 23, 25*br*, 28, 29*l* ZEFA; 29*t* Paul Brierley; 35*br*, 36*l* Mansell Collection; 39*l*, 39*r* 41*c*, 41*b* Philips; 41*t* Standard Telephones and Cables; 43*l* Philips; 43*r* Sony (UK); 44*t*, 44*r*, 46*t*, 46*b* Mansell Collection; 47*l* ZEFA; 47*r* Philips; 48*l*, 48*r* ZEFA; 49*t* Philips; 49*c*, 49*r* BLA; 51*br* Philips; 52, 53*tl*, 53*r* Philips; 54*t* NASA; 55*l*, 56*l*, 56*r* ZEFA; 58 United Nations; 58*b* Philips; 60 Michael Holford; 61 Colorsport.

Contents

NOTE TO THE READER: while you are reading this book you will notice that certain words appear in **bold type**. This is to indicate a word listed in the Glossary on page 62. This glossary gives brief explanations of words which may be new to you.

Introduction

Since the earliest times, human beings have always needed to pass on ideas, or **communicate**, with others. The first attempts were probably through gestures and grunts. One of the greatest steps forward in human development has been the growth of **language**. By language we mean a way of describing everything we see or do in words and sentences. The development of complex language is the single thing which sets humans apart from the rest of the animal kingdom. Our ability to exchange ideas and messages is the root of civilization. We spend more time communicating than on any other activity. Think of how much of your day is spent reading, talking, listening to music or radio, or watching television. All these are forms of communication. If we stop doing all these things we soon lose track of what is going on around us.

In the living world there are many different kinds of language and ways of communicating. All animals can pass on their feelings of anger, fear, pleasure or warning to others. We usually think of language as a series of noises and many animals do use sound for communicating. The chirp of a grasshopper and the bellow of a bull are typical of the language of animals. However, not all language depends upon sound. Many animals from the tiniest ant to the largest elephant use the language of smell. They leave scent messages on the ground to tell others of their presence. Even plants can communicate. They have special chemicals that are released inside or outside the plant. Some plants have sweet-smelling flowers to inform insects that they are there. Other plants produce chemicals from their roots to prevent overcrowding by informing their neighbours to keep their distance. In all these examples, language and communication help to produce order from the chaos of life.

The distance over which humans can communicate has increased greatly since the earliest time. Our voices only carry a mile or so even under ideal conditions. Drum beats carry a few miles further. The light from fires can travel up to fifty miles to give warnings. Modern communication relies on radio waves to carry

Have you ever thought what a wonderful thing the brain is? It starts working for us the moment we are born. Soon we are making simple sounds and in time these become words. Language grows and with language we can communicate with others. A year or two later, like the children in this picture, we start learning to read. Strangely enough, no one has yet been able to explain completely how children learn to read. We still have many unsolved mysteries and this is one of them.

voices or pictures in the form of an electronic 'language'. We have developed this type of communication to such an extent that we can now keep in contact with unmanned spacecraft millions of miles out in space.

Despite this leap in technology, most of our communication equipment is based upon our eyes, ears and **vocal cords**. The camera closely resembles the eye in the way that it produces a picture. The **loudspeaker** produces sounds in a similar way to our voices. The **microphone** collects sound waves and turns them into electrical **impulses** just as our ears do.

Without language we would have little of the quality of life and knowledge that we have in the world today. If we were unable to communicate with one another, using language, we would never be able to pass on knowledge or experience.

Airports use a radar system to plot the position of incoming aircraft. The information is recorded on a screen as in this picture. The flight controller gives instructions to pilots by radio.

Onshore station in Scotland for communication with North Sea oil rigs.

Animal communication

'It is a very inconvenient habit of kittens' (said Lewis Carroll's Alice) 'that, whatever you say to them, they always purr. ... How can you talk with a person if they always say the same thing?' The kitten's purr meant that it was pleased to have Alice paying attention to it, and had nothing to do with her human conversation. But most animals do 'always say the same thing' in a particular situation. A kitten will always purr when it is content, and a lamb will always call to its mother with the same bleat.

Animals do not have 'conversations' like humans. A chimpanzee may watch a beetle with great interest, but could not describe what it had seen to other chimpanzees. Chimpanzees communicate using many **gestures** and sounds but these are all concerned with their everyday needs and feelings.

Gestures, touch and facial expressions are more important to groups of apes and monkeys than the various sounds they use. Chimpanzees' faces can show fear, anger and amusement. They use many gestures that are the same as ours. They shake their fists and stamp their feet to show anger. Some gestures which seem similar to our own do in fact mean the opposite. A chimpanzee that appears to be smiling

is really terrified and showing its teeth as a warning. If they feel sorry for another chimpanzee they will pat it or cuddle it. Grooming each other is a sign of friendship and is done to strengthen family ties.

Apes such as gorillas and chimpanzees also signal to each other by the way they walk or stand. If the leader of a group of gorillas wants the group to move to a new feeding place he stands quite still, facing in the direction the others should take.

For birds, sound is most important, and they often have many different calls. The Great Tit, for example, uses more than fifty. Short, simple calls are used between parents and young, and as alarm signals. Some birds have special calls that imitate the animal that is threatening them. When a hen gives its danger signal, unhatched chicks (who cheep inside their eggs) stay quiet and still by **instinct.**

A bird usually takes over its own area for feeding and nesting. This is called its **territory.** The bird's song is a way of telling others where it is and where its territory begins and ends. Male birds also sing to attract females to mate. Pairs of birds will often sing together, one answering the other. Their long and complicated songs may have meanings that we have not yet worked out.

In the large colonies made by gannets, the nests are very close to one another. The territory of each pair is carefully guarded. When the parent birds return from getting food they have no difficulty in finding their young.

Dolphins *(right)* produce a variety of sounds. Some of these sounds are thought to be warning cries. They make other sounds which may be call signs so that dolphins can recognise each other at a distance.

The mandrill *(left)* is one of the most vicious of the primates. The male's brightly coloured face acts as a warning to other males and as a means of attracting females.

Birds are not the only animals to call just to tell each other they are there. Colonies of sea lions do this. So do flocks of sheep. Mother sheep have a special call that only their own lambs recognize.

We do not know why whales sing, but their underwater songs of growls and rumbles sometimes last for many hours. The patterns of notes are different for each individual, and perhaps they sing to let other whales know who and where they are.

Dolphins have a range of at least twenty different sounds. Experiments have been done to see if they use these noises as part of a language. However, no one has yet been able to prove that this is true. They certainly use sounds to say where they are and for warnings and alarms.

Smell is an important means of animal communication, though it is hard for us to understand as we are no good at it. Many mammals leave scent marks around their territory, as we might leave written messages, for others to find. When dogs meet they sniff each other. By doing this they recognize the owner of each different scent they come across.

Insect colonies are controlled by very powerful scents called **pheromones.** A female moth sends out a particular pheromone from special glands in her body. These strong scents can attract males from as far away as eight kilometres. Scientists can now make artificial pheromones which attract males of moths that are pests. The unlucky males are caught in a

trap and the female moths are unable to mate and lay eggs.

Ants and termites leave trails of pheromone leading to a source of food. As long as the food lasts they lay the scent on the way back, so the trail goes on getting stronger until the food runs out. Ants also have a fear scent. Worker ants react to this by moving towards it to help sort out the trouble.

Bees, who fly to their food, cannot lay trails. Instead, a bee who has found some nectar flies back to the hive to perform a dance which will tell the others where the food is. A 'round dance' means the food is nearby, but if it is more than one hundred metres away the bee does a 'tail-wagging dance'. The speed of the waggle tells the other bees the distance of the food from the hive. The bee also shows the other bees the direction in which to fly to find the food. The dance is complicated, but it shows what very good instinctive navigators bees are.

The male tussor silk moth. The giant antennae, looking like aerials, are used by the males to sense the pheromones given out by females when they are ready to mate.

Bees have a secret language which they use to show other bees a source of nectar. When the nectar is nearby they do a round dance. When it is more than 100 metres away they do a figure of eight dance. The distance is indicated by the number of turns a bee makes. The bee heads in a definite direction when wagging her abdomen and this is related to the position of the Sun. She shows the other bees how to find the nectar. They navigate by using the Sun as a marker.

The human nervous system

DO YOU EVER WONDER why a pin feels sharp and a rubber ball soft? This 'feeling' or sense of touch is just one of five basic senses, the others being taste, smell, sight and hearing.

Messages from the outside world are first received by tiny **receptor** cells. These special cells may be in our skin, mouth, nose, eyes or deep within our ears. These messages, or **stimuli**, need to reach our brain to be interpreted as sensations. The nervous system is like a telephone network with the brain as the exchange to which all calls lead. Throughout our body are millions of tiny nerves which are the 'local lines' of the telephone system. These lead to the **spinal cord** which is the 'trunk line'. This, in turn, goes directly to the brain. Unlike the telephone exchange, the brain decides how important the 'calls' or stimuli are and if our bodies should do anything about them.

The brain and spinal cord make up what we call the **central nervous system.** The nerves that carry messages to and from the brain are part of the **peripheral nervous system.**

One of the simplest examples of how the nervous system works is to think of what happens when we are pricked by a pin. As the pin pushes into our finger a tiny pressure-sensitive cell, or receptor, is pressed. This sets up a signal or **impulse** in a nerve fibre. This fibre is part of a special cell called a **neuron** or nerve cell which is shaped like a tiny, long electric cable. Each nerve contains many neurons. The conducting wire, or **axon** of each neuron carries the impulse to the spinal cord. Inside the spine the message is passed on to other neurons, one of which runs back to our arm muscle. The muscle is known as an **effector**, meaning that it puts the messages sent by the neuron into effect.

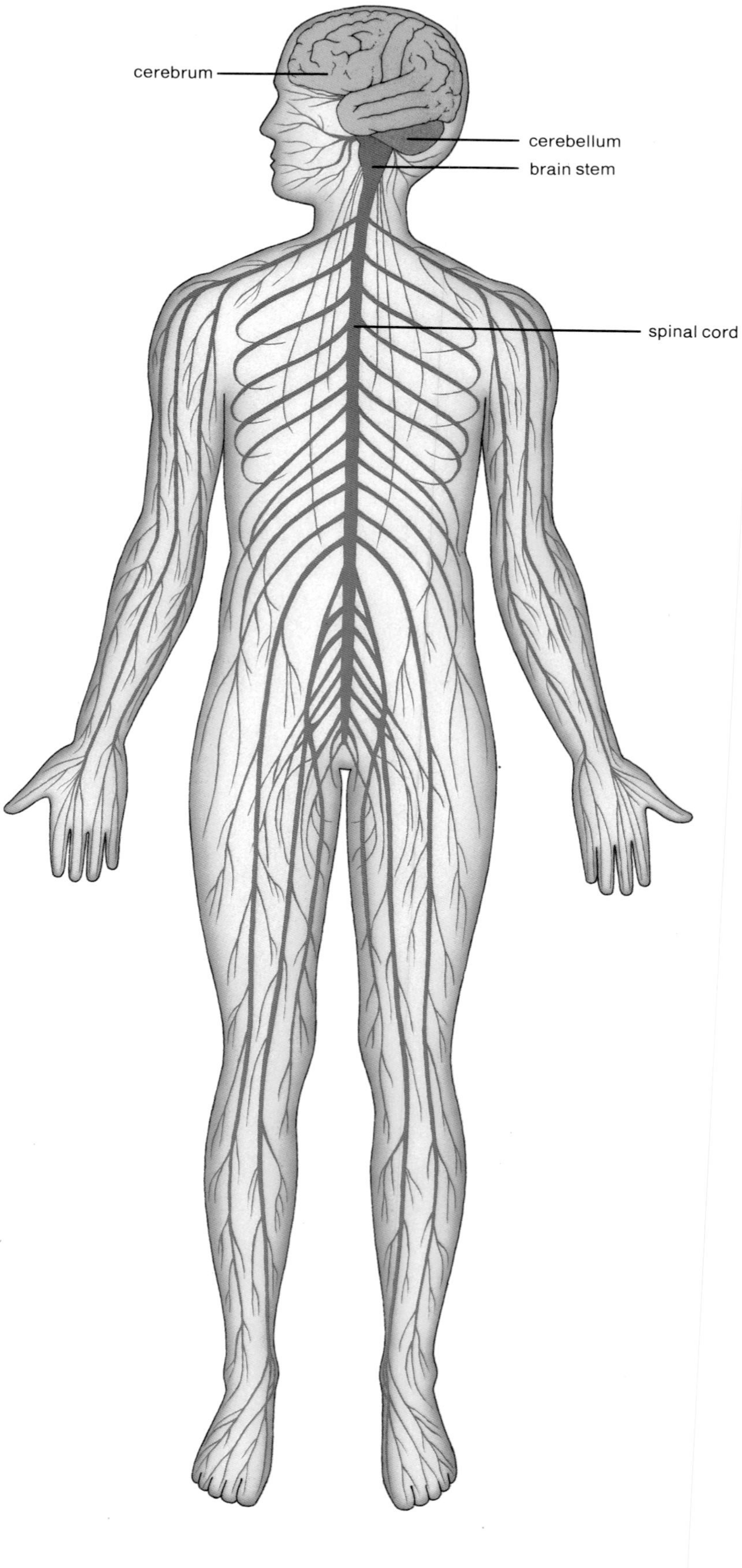

cerebrum

cerebellum

brain stem

spinal cord

The human nervous system consists of millions of nerve cells. The brain and the spinal cord make up the central nervous system. All the nerves emerging from the brain and spinal cord form the peripheral nervous system. These nerves act as receivers and transmitters of messages. Our five senses, and all actions of the body, depend on these messages.

When we are pricked by a pin, we respond with a reflex action. An impulse passes down a nerve fibre to the spinal cord. From there one message is sent to the brain, and one is sent back down the arm. This makes the muscle jerk our hand away.

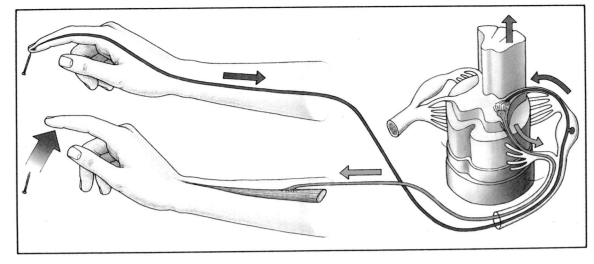

A nerve is a bundle of nerve cells, called neurons. There are millions of neurons in the human body, mostly in the brain. In a single neuron the receptors pass the information to the cell body through a long fibre, the axon. Axons are covered by a fatty substance which insulates and protects the nerve fibre.

When the impulse reaches the arm, it makes the muscles pull our hand away from the pin. This is known as a **reflex action.** As a result we move our arm away before we 'feel' the pain.

The impulse sent to our spinal cord also sends a message up the spine to the brain. This tells us that our finger has been pricked and the brain tells our eyes to look for the pin. Other instructions sent out by the brain make us yell out and suck the wounded finger.

A SINGLE NEURON

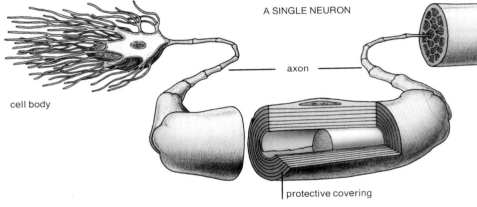

cell body

axon

a bundle of neurons

protective covering

Various areas of the brain have different functions. The largest part of the brain is the cerebrum. This is where most of your advanced thinking takes place.

The left hemisphere. This side of the brain is responsible for such things as speech, hearing, reading, writing and seeing.

The brain is made up of three main parts. The largest, the **cerebrum**, is split into two halves or **lobes.** Here all the messages from the outside world are collected together. The main senses are dealt with in this part of the brain. Messages from the right side of the body are sent to the left half of the brain and vice versa. Thus a pin prick in our left hand is sensed in the right half of our brain. Each sense, touch, taste and smell, hearing or sight, is dealt with in separate parts within the cerebrum. If the brain is damaged on the right side then some of the senses on the left half of our body may be affected.

Below the cerebrum, at the back of the brain, is the smaller **cerebellum**, a round ball of nerve cells. The cerebellum controls our movements and balance. Deep inside the brain, where it joins the spinal cord, is the **brain stem.** This controls our **autonomic nervous system** which is like the automatic pilot control of an aircraft. The brain stem controls our body temperature, breathing, heartbeat and other vital systems without our knowing it. Imagine the strain of having to keep thinking about how fast to make your heart beat or how to keep your body temperature constant!

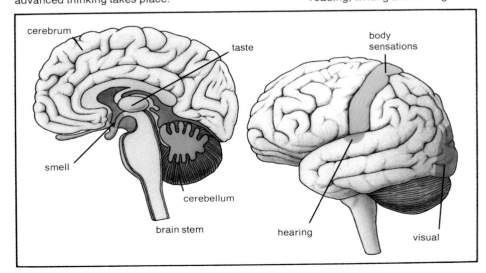

cerebrum

taste

body sensations

smell

cerebellum

brain stem

hearing

visual

Hearing and balance

HEARING is one of the five senses. The others are sight, touch, taste and smell. We sense sounds by means of our ears which pick up vibrations in the air and change them into nerve signals. These signals go to the brain and then we hear the sounds.

The visible part of the ear, called the **pinna**, funnels sound waves down the **auditory passage** to the **eardrum**. The sound waves make the eardrum vibrate or move in and out very quickly. In the middle ear are three very small ear-bones called the **hammer**, **anvil** and **stirrup**. The vibration of the eardrum makes the ear-bones move. They are arranged to make the vibrations twenty times larger, and these vibrations reach the **cochlea** in the inner ear.

The cochlea is filled with liquid and the vibrations make this move. Inside the cochlea are fibres which are connected to nerve endings. These fibres pick up movements of the liquid and send messages to the brain through the **auditory nerve**.

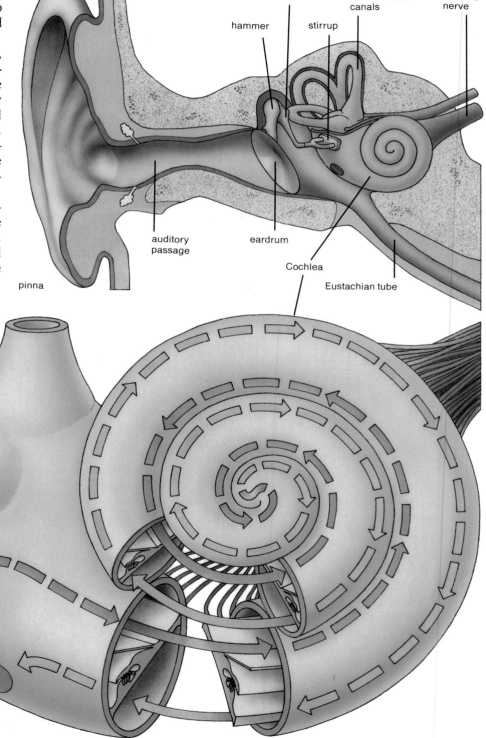

hammer · anvil · stirrup · semi-circular canals · auditory nerve

auditory passage · eardrum · Cochlea · Eustachian tube

pinna

oval window

round window

Vibrations can also travel through water where sound waves travel about four and a half times faster than in air. Human ears do not work well under water but fish have very good hearing. Their inner ears are similar to ours but sound waves reach them by travelling through the whole body of the fish. Fish do not have a special auditory passage.

Also in the inner ear are the **semi-circular canals**. These have nothing to do with hearing. They are used to help the body keep itself balanced. Imagine carrying a bowl of water. If you turn a corner, the bowl turns but the water does not. If the bowl could 'feel' the water it would notice this happening itself. The semi-circular canals work in this way and are filled with liquid. When your head turns the liquid tends to stay still as in the case of the bowl of water. Nerve endings in the canals pick up this information and send messages to the brain. There are three different canals each of which respond to different movements.

Think of the bowl of water again. If you kept on turning it, after a time the water would start spinning too. Stop the bowl rotating and the liquid carries on spinning a bit longer. This is rather like what happens when we make ourselves dizzy. Spin round for a long time and the liquid in your semi-circular canals starts spinning too. When you stop, the liquid carries on moving. Because the canal is still it 'notices' the liquid moving, so it tells your brain you are spinning even though you are standing still. This is why you feel dizzy.

The middle ear is joined to the back of the nose by a passage called the **Eustachian tube**. This tube opens when we swallow and lets air from the nose pass into the middle ear. Because air from the outside is always pressing on the eardrum, there must be air on the inside as well. Otherwise the eardrum would be pushed inwards, and would not be able to vibrate. The purpose of the Eustachian tube is to equalize air pressure on either side of the eardrum.

You will notice this if you travel by aeroplane. As the aeroplane takes off and

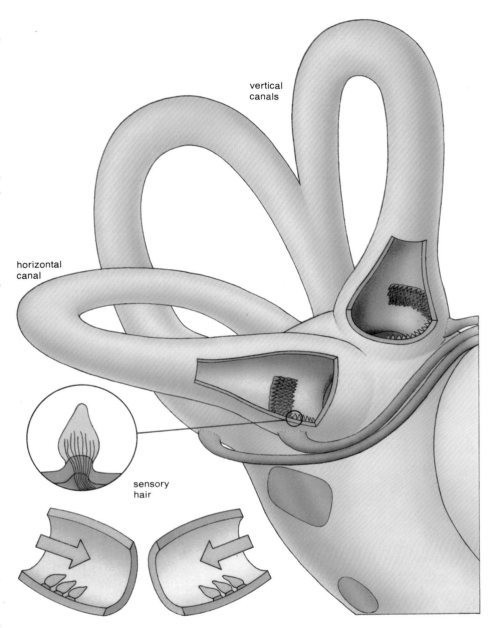

vertical canals

horizontal canal

sensory hair

Sound waves enter the ear through the auditory passage. The canal is protected by tiny hairs and wax. These trap dust and prevent it from reaching the eardrum. The eardrum is a membrane or thin sheet of skin at the end of the canal. The sound waves make your eardrum vibrate. The inner ear converts the vibrations into electrical signals. They go to the brain through the auditory nerve.

climbs, the air pressure on the outside of your eardrum gets lower. The middle ear is closed, and so the pressure in it does not change. The result is that the air outside pushes the eardrum inwards and stops it vibrating. This causes slight deafness or even earache. Normally, you can cure this by swallowing. This opens the Eustachian tube and allows the air pressure on either side of the eardrum to become equal. The reverse happens when the aeroplane lands.

If you have a head cold, the Eustachian tube and the middle ear can sometimes get filled with mucus. This can block the Eustachian tube and stop the pressure equalization taking place even if you swallow hard. The mucus can also drag on the three ear-bones. This can stop them vibrating and cause slight deafness.

The inner ear as well as letting you hear also helps you to keep your balance. In the inner ear there are three semi-circular canals which contain fluid. Each canal is positioned at a different plane. They are like the spirit levels which builders use. In each of the three organs of balance there are sensory hairs which notice every movement you make. They pass signals to your brain which tells your body to make correcting movements.

The vocal organs and speech

YOU MIGHT THINK that speaking comes naturally like seeing and hearing. Yet it is not something you can do soon after you are born. Speech is not one of the five senses, and it has to be learnt during the first few years of life.

All babies cry in the first few seconds or minutes after birth. Crying is the first use of the vocal organs and the first step towards speaking. Very soon babies start to coo, gurgle and babble. Babbling sounds like talking, but not in any particular language.

Crying is the first step towards speaking. The baby is using the vocal organs from the moment of birth. As the baby grows, sounds and simple words begin to develop, by imitation.

Gradually a baby learns to recognise each pattern of sound, to find out what it means and to copy it. A baby's first words are learnt by imitating the simple words used by the mother and other members of the family. Babies who hear two languages being spoken all the time, such as English and French, are able to learn words in both languages at the same time. They may grow up to be **bilingual.**

You can see how important it is for babies to be able to hear properly. If they cannot, they are unable to imitate sounds and words so that they will be very slow learning to speak. Babies suffering from deafness need to have hearing aids fitted as soon as possible, otherwise speech will be very slow to develop.

By the time you were five years old you were probably using about 2000 words. As well, you knew the meaning of several thousand more when you heard other people using them. While your memory was storing away the words and rules of grammar, you were also learning to make all the different sounds you need for speech. There are about forty of these sounds. We use them in speech in the same way that we use letters of the alphabet for making written words.

Speech appears to be controlled by just one-half of the brain, usually the left side. A small section of the brain called **Broca's area** seems to play an important part in controlling the vocal organs. These are the parts of the body we use when we speak. Another section of the left half of the brain, called **Wernicke's area** acts as a memory store for language.

The vocal organs all do other jobs too, such as breathing, tasting and eating, but in humans

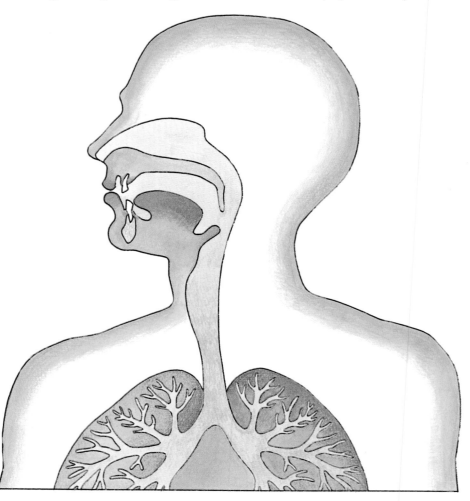

Simplified diagram to show the speech organs.
When we speak, air from the lungs passes through the larynx to make sounds. The sounds are changed into words by different organs, the nasal passage, the lips, the teeth, the tongue and the palate. All of these organs serve other purposes than speech.

they are shaped to make speech easy. Monkeys, for example, have long thin tongues while the human tongue is short and thick. This helps us to change the shape of the space in our mouths when making different sounds.

The first thing you need for speech is breath, which comes from your lungs. Before you say anything your brain works out how much breath you will need to take in. As you start to breathe out, the air arrives at your **larynx**. This is like two doors of muscles at the front of your throat, in your Adam's apple. The edges of the doors are the **vocal cords.** They are normally open, but when you speak they close, until air forces them apart and a tiny puff of air escapes.

The cords close and open again and again, to cause a **vibration.** Put your finger on your Adam's apple and say 'Oh'. You should be able to feel the vibration that is making the sound. The larynx controls the loudness and **pitch** of your voice (whether it is high or low).

The sounds are shaped into words in your **vocal tract.** This is the passage the sound follows until it escapes from your lips. It goes through the **pharynx**, the space behind the tongue, into your mouth, and also up into your nose. For **vowel** sounds the tract is open. Try saying 'eye', 'ah', 'you', 'oh', and feel how your mouth and throat change shape for each sound.

Most words are vowel sounds and **consonants** combined. Try 'if', 'ash', 'the', 'zoo', 'lie'. You make these sounds by pushing air through a narrow gap in your vocal tract. For example, the 'f' sound is made between your upper teeth and lower lip. With your tongue behind your upper teeth you get 'th'. For some other consonants you close the tract completely and cause a tiny explosion of air. If you say the word 'paddock' you should be able to feel three explosions, each in a different place in your mouth.

The consonants in 'mining' are all nasal, made in the nose. To say this your mouth is shut off from the vocal tract by your **soft palate.** You can feel this with your tongue behind your **hard palate**, the roof of your mouth.

The vocal organs in open and closed positions. During normal breathing the vocal cords are open. When we speak they are brought together by muscles. Air from the lungs is forced through the narrow gap, making the cords vibrate. The quicker the air is pushed through, the louder the voice sounds. The tension of the cords controls pitch; the slacker they are the lower the note, as in a stringed instrument. If they are tight the note will be high. The final sound we make further depends on the shape of the mouth and lips.

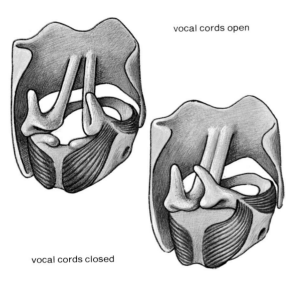

vocal cords open

vocal cords closed

People who are deaf have to rely on lip-reading to understand what others are saying. The lips take up different positions for each sound. See if you can lip-read each of the simple vowel sounds in the picture.

How language began

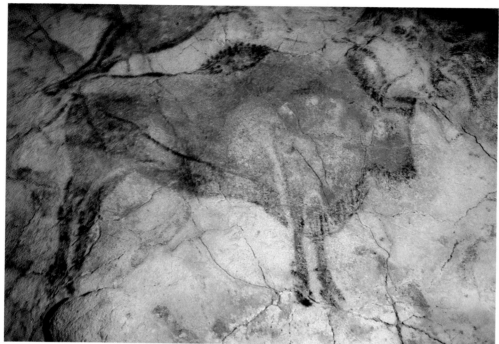

SPOKEN LANGUAGE is so old that we have to guess how it began. The first people to speak to each other probably lived at least one million years ago. They were **nomads**. This means they hunted animals for food and travelled around in search of them. They lived in small groups, and shared out the work they had to do to stay alive. The men made knives and spearheads out of stones, and went hunting. The women probably collected fruit and water, and looked after the children.

Like other animals who live in groups our ancestors would have used calls and other sounds to communicate. They also learnt to make each different noise stand for a single object or idea. They would have given names to the desert, the forest, the sky, day and night, the weather, food, water, plants and animals. They would also have made words for what they did, hunting, running, sleeping or eating.

All they knew had to be remembered. To help them, and to teach the children, they probably made up songs, dances and rituals that they performed whenever anything important happened, like someone dying or being born, or rain falling after dry weather. The group's language and its traditions (its **culture**) helped to keep its members together.

Painting of a bison from the caves of Altamira, North Spain. Wall paintings like this one were made by cave-dwellers, thousands of years ago. These pictures are thought to have had a magic meaning for hunters, but no one really knows.

If you could not read, you would be able to tell what this book is about by looking at the pictures on each page. Pictures are a kind of language. Some of the oldest pictures were painted about 30 000 years ago on the walls of caves. They are usually of animals, and many are very beautiful. No one knows why they were painted. They may have been a record of what was hunted, or perhaps the hunter thought that if he painted a deer or a buffalo it would work as a kind of magic to help him find the real animals.

While artists were at work on these cave paintings, another sort of 'drawing' was also used. Dots and dashes were scratched on sticks and bones as a way of counting and keeping records. Some of them may have been used as calendars, for counting days and showing the **phases** of the moon. Both the paintings and the stick-records show that by this time people had worked out how to make **symbols** of the world around them.

Sumerian tablet about 2800 BC. This shows the pictographic signs which were the beginning of written language.

Pictures show objects and actions, and writing really began with them. The little 'matchstick' drawings the first writers used are called **pictographs.** But try drawing this message: 'Please lend me a pen until tomorrow. I've left mine at home'. You can draw yourself, your friend, the pen, your home. However, can you draw 'lend', 'tomorrow' and 'left'? Can you also draw 'please'?

You could do it if you could use pictures that stood for the sounds of the words. Such signs are **phonetic.** They can represent sounds in the exact order in which they are spoken. Using pictures, you can write down what you can see. If you use sound signs you can write down your ideas and feelings, and you can write all the 'connecting' words that make sentences.

The first people to write in pictographs, about 5 000 years ago, were the Sumerians. They lived in Mesopotamia in the Middle East. By now, cities were being built and the people were becoming farmers, craftsmen, merchants, priests. They had kings and they had to pay taxes, and all needed to keep records of what they were doing. Sometimes they wanted to communicate with people in other cities, so they had to send letters. They wrote these on clay tablets. Many of the phonetic signs they used were based on objects whose names sounded like the words they wanted to write.

Some languages are still written in pictographs today. The Chinese and Japanese use symbols which are usually called **characters.** Each character stands for a whole word. New characters have had to be devised to express new ideas, and today there are several thousand Chinese characters in use.

Our ancestors roamed around in groups hunting for wild animals and gathering fruit and berries. Looking at a scene like this, you can imagine them making various sounds to each other. They would have made special sounds for each kind of animal, and sounds meaning excitement and danger. This was how language began.

Writing and alphabets

PICTURE LANGUAGES are difficult to learn because the symbol for each word has to be memorized. Although many of the people of the Ancient World needed to use written languages, very few learnt to write themselves. Instead, they paid **scribes** to write for them.

The scribes probably began learning to write when quite young and would go on learning until they were sixteen or eighteen years old. They were often the sons and daughters of scribes who passed down their skill. If not, they went to school much as we do now. Writing seemed mysterious and strange to people who could not do it, and the scribes became important and respected.

A scribe needed a tool and a surface to write on. Various materials were used and this affected the appearance of the writing. In Sumeria the signs were pressed into soft clay with a stick (or **stylus**) which made wedge-shaped marks. The writing came to be known as **cuneiform**, meaning wedge-shaped.

In China the oldest writing that has been found was cut into metal or shell, and the pictographs are made of straight lines. But later the Chinese scribes used ink and brushes, and wrote on silk. The straight lines were turned into curves by the brush and the characters appear soft and flowing.

The Egyptians invented a set of pictographs in about 3000BC. These were often used in carvings on their tombs and temples, and they are called **hieroglyphs**, which means 'holy carvings'. You can see from the picture that the shapes are stiff and like stone.

The Egyptian scribes needed another writing material which could be carried around. They used squares of wood, but their most important invention was paper. They made it from a type of rush plant called **papyrus** that grew in the swamps around the River Nile. The stems of the plant were beaten into thin strips. They were laid edge to edge and a second layer of strips was pasted across them. Then the whole sheets were beaten flat and rubbed smooth with a stone before being joined together into a long roll of paper. The scribes wrote with a reed dipped in paint. They chewed the tip of the reed so that it worked like a tiny brush.

Another, even greater, invention was needed

Egyptian workers harvesting papyrus, a straw-like reed which grew thickly in the Nile Valley.

Thin strips of pith from the stem of the papyrus reed being beaten together to form paper.

The single sheets of paper were pasted together to form long rolls.

This picture on papyrus, now in the British Museum, shows the mummy of an important person being drawn by oxen to the burial place. Beneath the picture are hieroglyphs proclaiming the life and deeds of the person who has died.

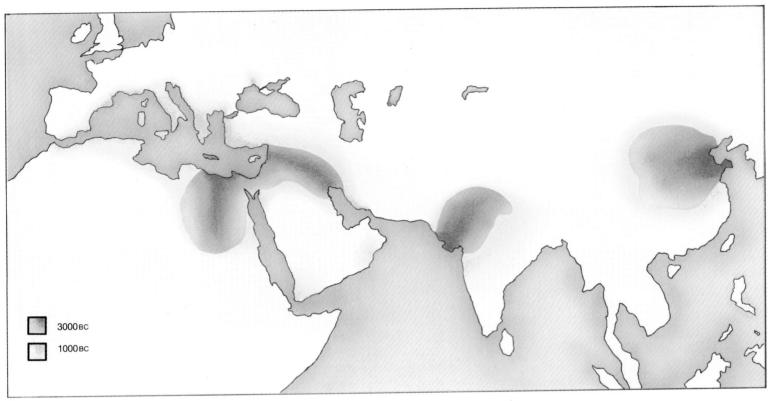

This map shows how reading and writing spread after the development of the first alphabets. Between 3000 and 1000BC there were four main centres where these skills were in use. In the Middle East there were two centres, the Nile Valley and the land around the Tigris and Euphrates rivers. In Asia there were also two centres, the Indus river in India and the fertile plains of China.

After 1000BC reading and writing spread from the Middle East to Europe as a result of seafaring and trading in the Mediterranean. The Chinese, however, continued to use symbols which are usually called characters. They did not adopt an alphabet and the Chinese language still uses pictographs rather than letters.

to make writing really useful for everyone. This was the alphabet. Seven alphabets are used in the world today, but they are all based on the same idea of a set of signs, each standing for a single sound. These can be used in any order to make any word. They are not quite perfect, and one sign sometimes has to stand for more than one sound (for instance, 'c' in 'court' and 'palace'). This depends on how the letters are mixed up. But if you see a word written for the first time you can usually tell how it sounds if you know the rules.

The Phoenicians were a group of people who lived on the eastern shore of the Mediterranean Sea. Their land was poor and so, instead of farming, they became traders. They sailed all round the Mediterranean, and met people from every other Middle Eastern city. As a result, they learnt many different languages and new ideas. Cuneiform and hieroglyphs had been used for more than a thousand years, and

though they were still used for important documents, the scribes no longer had time to use them for everything.

By 1000BC the Phoenicians had an alphabet which they spread everywhere. In the East it became Aramaic, an ancient language from which Indian, Persian, Arabic and Hebrew grew. In the West the Phoenicians taught their alphabet to the Greeks.

At this time the alphabet had twenty-two characters, all **consonants.** The Greeks added five **vowels.** These sounds you make with little or no use of your tongue or lips. The Latin alphabet is adapted from Greek and is the one used for western European languages, such as English. Cyrillic, the Russian alphabet, comes from Greek too.

The alphabet made writing much easier and meant that many more people could learn to do it. Reading and writing at last became useful tools for all kinds of communication.

The development of the alphabet. This table shows how three of our letters, A, H and S gradually changed from early times to the present day.

early Phoenician	early Hebrew	Moabite	Phoenician	early Greek	classical Greek	classical Etruscan	classical Latin	modern capitals
K	F	K	∢	⊿	A	A	A	A
⊟	⊞	⋈	⋈	⊟	H	⊟	H	H
W	W	W	W	≶	Σ	≶	S	S

The first printing

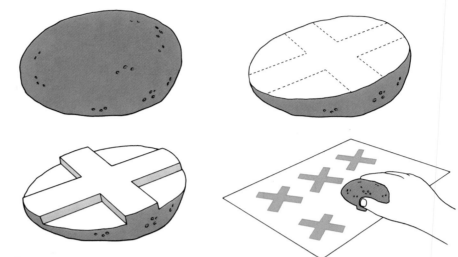

MODERN BOOKS, like this one, are published in **editions** of thousands of copies, so that everyone who wishes to can read them. Every copy is exactly alike, but until about five hundred years ago books were written out by hand and each copy was different. This took a lot of time and skill, so that books were very scarce and expensive. Most people never saw a book and could not read.

From about the year 1200, universities began to be set up in Europe and the students needed books to study. As the number of students grew the need for books increased. The scribes, who wrote the books by hand, could not keep up with the demand.

In Europe, scribes wrote on parchment of vellum, stiff sheets made from animal skins. After 1400 they began to use paper instead, which was cheaper and easier to produce. Paper had first been made centuries earlier in China. In the British Museum there is a letter written on Chinese paper made before AD 137. However, the invention took a very long time to reach Europe.

The early paper-makers used rags soaked in a solution of lime. They pounded the mixture to separate the **fibres** and make a soupy liquid. A mould made of wire mesh in a frame was dipped into the tub and lifted out. The water drained away leaving a thin layer of fibres. They were squeezed between cloth to flatten them into a sheet of paper.

Some books were printed using wooden **blocks.** You can make a block by drawing a picture on a flat surface, such as a potato cut in half, and by cutting away the background. You dab ink over the block and press it down on paper. The picture which you get is called an **impression** and it is a mirror-image of the one on the block. The block can be used a number of times and the impression will be the same with each printing.

The Chinese made the first block-printed books, and the oldest one which still exists was made in AD 868. It is called the Diamond Sutra and is a roll of seven sheets of paper, each printed from one block.

Block-printing in Europe was mainly used for playing cards and books of religious pictures with only a few words. In about 1450 a new idea made it possible to print the books that had always been written out by hand before.

The first person to do this was probably a German goldsmith called Johann Gensfleisch zum Gutenberg. He worked out how to use a separate block for each letter. Before the book was printed, the letters could be changed or moved around to correct mistakes. Gutenberg was using **movable type.**

It is quite simple to make a printing block using a potato. Cut the potato in half and draw the design you want to print. Then cut away sections of potato to leave the raised design. Dab ink on the raised part and press it down on paper.

Before printing began everything had to be written by hand. The people who did this work were known as scribes, and the work was known as a manuscript (from the Latin, meaning 'handwritten'). This beautiful early manuscript *(left)* is dated about 1350.

If you look down this page you will see that the same letters are used many times over. For Gutenberg's method to work he needed hundreds of pieces of type for each letter. They all had to fit together to make an absolutely flat printing surface. This meant all the pieces had to be the same height. The answer was to cast the type in metal. This means pouring molten (melted) metal into a mould, where it cools and hardens. Every piece of type from the same mould is exactly the same height. The mould for each letter is called the **matrix.**

The next thing Gutenberg needed was ink. The kind used for writing was watery and would not stick properly to metal type. However, some years earlier artists had begun to use oil paints. The Flemish painters were the first to do this, led by Jan van Eyck. Gutenberg copied the idea and mixed pigment (colouring material) with oil to make thick, sticky printing ink.

Printers use a printing press to bring the type and the paper together. In Gutenberg's press the type was laid face up on a 'flat bed'. The paper was laid on top of the type. Another flat board, called the **platen**, was pressed down hard on top of the paper to make the impression.

Early wooden block used for making playing cards.

Johann Gutenberg, 1394–1468. Born in Mainz in Germany, he invented movable type.

The Marriage of Arnolfini by Jan van Eyck. Van Eyck was one of the first painters to use oil paints. Gutenberg copied the idea and used oil to thicken his printing inks.

This old picture of a sixteenth century printing works shows people setting type, inking up, printing and checking the proofs. The Latin inscription on the picture reads as follows: 'It is possible for one message to reach many ears: this is the way they smear ink on to a thousand pages from one manuscript'.

The first book to be printed using movable type was a bible published in 1456. Forty-seven copies of this book still exist today. No one knows how much of it was printed by Gutenberg himself, but it is usually known as the Gutenberg Bible. William Caxton, the first English printer, started printing in London in 1476.

Soon after this, a number of presses began to appear. One of the first was Cambridge University Press, which was formed in 1534, only fifty or sixty years after Gutenberg and Caxton.

From words to print

THE PROCESS which Gutenberg used to print his books is called letterpress. In this process the raised surface of the type and illustrations is inked and pressed against single sheets of paper.

To arrange the type for a book every letter was picked up separately and arranged in order in a composing stick, a small tray which could hold a few lines of type. The person who did the typesetting was called a **compositor**. Each line was spaced out and adjusted to fit the page to be printed.

When the stick was full the lines of type were moved to a larger tray called a **galley**. Galleys held several pages of type in a long column. The compositor had to space out the lines by using extra strips of metal called **leads.** These did not print because they were lower than the raised type; they appeared as space between the lines on the page.

The type in the galley was inked and a copy made on a sheet of paper. This copy, called a

The compositor is taking type from the typecase and placing it in a composing stick.

A range of varied typefaces, including Photina which is the one used for the main text in this book.

proof, was used to check that there were no mistakes. Once the type was correct it was divided into pages and these were arranged in a metal frame called a **chase**. If the book was to have pictures they would be printed from blocks placed in the right positions in the chase. The type was then locked up with pieces of wood and metal, called **furniture**, so that none of the pieces could fall out. The whole thing was called a **forme**. This forme was then transferred to a printing machine, inked, and printed on to the paper.

For five centuries letterpress printing was almost the only method of printing books or any other printed matter.

Printers now use alphabets of many different shapes and sizes, as you will see from looking at books or magazines. The whole range of a particular design is called a **typeface**. Each typeface has a name and the one used for the main text in this book is called 'Photina'. To begin with the designs were based on styles of handwriting. The most important thing about a typeface is that it must be easy to read.

At the end of the last century the invention of a composing machine made typesetting much faster. The compositor used a keyboard like that of a typewriter. On the first machine, the Linotype machine, the compositor 'typed' out a complete line, which was then cast in metal by the machine. The next machine, the Monotype machine, cast each letter separately and then arranged them in order. Machines like these are still being used today in many parts of the world.

The next development was phototypesetting. In this method the operator still uses a keyboard, but the letters are enlarged to the right size and exposed on film or photographic paper. Text for a whole book can be sent by post to be

Compositor at a Linotype machine. In this machine a complete line of type was cast in hot metal to make one block. After use the metal was melted down and used again.

printed thousands of miles away. The same text set in metal type could have weighed many tonnes.

Nowadays computer typesetting is widely used. The keyboard operator types out the copy. At the same time he inserts special codes which tell the computer what design and size of lettering is required, when to use capital letters, bold or italic letters and how to space out the lines. These words you are reading have been set on a computer typesetting machine.

Just as there have been great changes in typesetting so there have been in the printing processes. After five centuries of use letterpress printing has largely given way to two other methods of printing, **photogravure** and **lithography.**

In photogravure the opposite process to letterpress takes place. The letters or pictures to be printed are made up of holes (or cells) in the surface of a metal plate. This metal plate is curved around a cylinder. The cells are filled with ink and when pressed into contact with paper (in a roll), the letters and pictures are transferred. Photogravure printing is sometimes used for books but you will more often see it in colourful illustrated magazines.

This book has been printed by lithography, which is described on the following pages.

Golf ball and daisy wheel attachments are used on impact printers (typewriters) for computer printouts. On a golf ball the letters stand out from the surface of the ball. On a daisy wheel the letters are on the end of each spoke or petal. In both cases they print by hitting an inked ribbon.

How books are printed

LITHOGRAPHY is the printing process which is now used for printing most of the books you will read – and also all sorts of other printed matter.

You can discover the basic idea of the process by drawing a picture with a wax crayon. Try to paint over your drawing using watercolours. You will find that the watercolour paint soaks into the paper but does not change the lines of the picture you have drawn. This is because oil in the crayon and water in the paint do not mix.

Lithography was, and is still, used by artists to produce copies of their work. They draw or paint directly on to a specially smooth stone, using oil crayons or inks. The word lithography comes from the Greek words for 'stone' and 'drawing'.

When the picture is finished the stone is dampened. The oily parts, the lines of the drawing, stay dry. Printing ink is oily too, so when it is rolled on to the stone it sticks only to the drawing. Now paper can be laid over the stone and pressed down flat to make a copy or print.

This book was printed on the Roland 800 four-colour litho printing machine illustrated above.

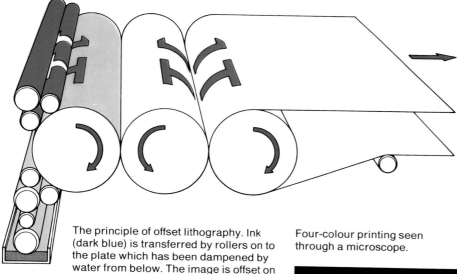

The principle of offset lithography. Ink (dark blue) is transferred by rollers on to the plate which has been dampened by water from below. The image is offset on to another roller and then printed on paper.

For printing books thin metal plates are used instead of stones, but the basic process is still the same. The words and pictures are reproduced on the printing plates using photographic processes.

The plate is wrapped around a cylinder on the lithographic printing press. It is then dampened and inked, just as the stone was dampened and inked. Next to the cylinder containing the plate is another cylinder, around which is wrapped a soft 'blanket'. When the two cylinders revolve against each other the words and pictures are transferred to the blanket. This, in turn, revolves against the paper which is curved around a third cylinder, called the impression cylinder. The words and pictures are printed on to the paper. The soft blanket is used so that every little detail on the printing plate is transferred to the paper. This type of lithographic printing is called '**offset**' lithography.

If single sheets of paper are used on the printing press the process is called sheet-fed offset. If a continuous roll (or reel) of paper is used, it is called web-offset. A machine using a roll of paper can print much faster than one using single sheets of paper.

If you have a close look at a black and white photograph you can see that the picture is made up of various greys. These range from almost white to dark grey and black. The printer, using only black ink, has difficulty in printing these continuous tones. To reproduce the photograph he has to break it up into small dots, by copying it through a fine screen. Where the black dots are close together the picture looks almost black. Light areas are made up of fewer dots. If you look at a photograph in a book or newspaper through a magnifying glass you will see the little dots. A picture made up in this way is called a **half-tone**.

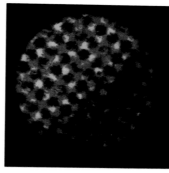

Four-colour printing seen through a microscope.

When colour illustrations are printed, four different inks have to be used. These inks are coloured yellow, cyan (blue), magenta (red) and black. One printing plate is made for each colour and arranged to print on the paper in a carefully chosen order. Together the four printings can produce practically any colour as you can see from the pictures in this book.

In four-colour printing separate plates have to be made for each colour. The colours used are yellow, cyan (blue), magenta (red) and black. On a four-colour printing machine the paper is fed from a large roll and passed over each plate in succession. The illustration taken from page 56, shows how the colour builds up as the sheet is fed through the machine.

23

Sound and how it travels

SOUND IS IMPORTANT to us since it allows us to communicate with each other. Some sounds are unpleasant to our ears and these we sometimes call noise. For example, we do not like the noise made by heavy traffic, or the noise of thunder.

All sounds, whether they are pleasant or unpleasant, are a form of energy created by vibrating objects. A **vibration** is a rapid movement backwards and forwards. The movement is usually so fast that it cannot be seen. For example, when we speak or sing, even when we whisper, our vocal cords vibrate. The vibrations cause pressure changes in the air around us and these spread out in the form of waves. These waves go in every direction. Even if you are standing with your back to someone, that person can hear you talking.

When we speak to someone our vocal cords vibrate, and these same vibrations are picked up by the other person's ear-drums, which also vibrate. Sound, therefore, can travel through air, but how does this happen? The air around us consists of millions and millions of tiny particles, which are known as air **molecules**. When an object vibrates, such as your vocal cords, it pushes the first layer of air molecules forward. These push on the second layer and bounce back slightly. The second layer hits the third layer and so on. A ripple of energy moves outwards, and reaches the ear of the person listening.

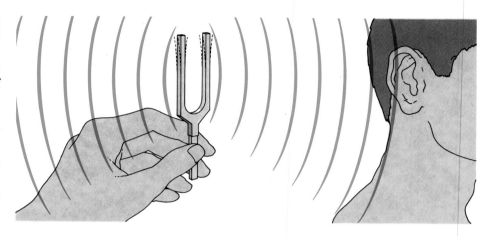

A tuning fork is metal and gives an exact musical note when struck. It helps people to tune musical instruments. It sends out vibrations which are received by the human ear. A piano-tuner hears the sound made by the tuning fork and adjusts the piano strings until the two sounds match each other.

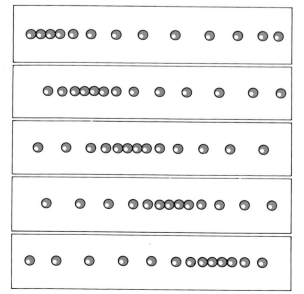

Sound waves disturb the molecules as they pass through air. The molecules knock into each other, vibrating backwards and forwards in a regular manner. The waves go through the air, but the air as a whole does not move.

This is how we communicate with each other. A person who is deaf is severely handicapped, since speech is our primary means of communication. The ears of a deaf person do not pick up the vibrations made by our vibrating vocal cords.

Sound waves can travel through other things in addition to air. They can travel through liquids such as water, and through solids such as metal pipes. Knock a water pipe in one part of the house and someone else can hear it in another part. However, sound cannot travel in a **vacuum**, that is to say in empty space, because there are no air molecules to carry the sound waves. This is why astronauts in space have to talk to each other by radio. Although radio waves can travel through space, sound waves cannot.

Sound takes time to travel from one place to another. Imagine you are on a sportsfield watching the start of a race. You see a puff of smoke as the starter fires the pistol, and you see the athletes starting to run. An instant later you hear the noise of the gun. This is because light travels much faster than sound. In the same way, in a thunderstorm you normally hear the thunder a few seconds after you see the lightning.

Sound travels in air at a speed of about 1 200 kilometres per hour at sea level. As the medium through which sound travels becomes denser, the speed becomes higher. In water, for example, sound travels at about four times the speed it does in air. Because the atmosphere becomes less dense the higher we go, the speed of sound is also reduced.

Mach 0·5

Mach 0·9

Mach 2

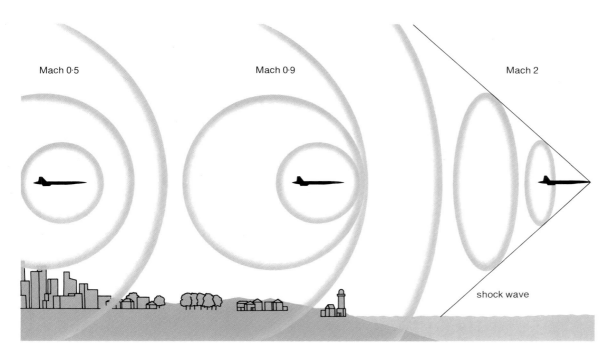

shock wave

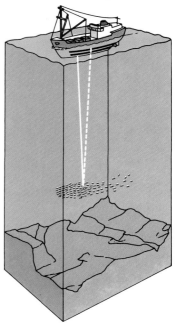

Ships use sonar (SOund Navigation And Ranging) to find the depth of the seabed beneath them by echo-sounding. The depth of the water is measured by the time taken for the echo to come back to the ship.

In **supersonic** aeroplanes, speed is generally measured by **Mach** numbers. Mach 1 is the speed of sound, whatever the altitude. When an aeroplane is travelling at Mach 2, it is travelling at twice the speed of sound, and so on. As an aeroplane approaches Mach 1, strange things happen. First, there is buffeting, and shock waves build up over the airframe. As it passes Mach 1 a shock wave is formed causing the sonic boom which sounds like an explosion. This can cause damage to buildings on the ground. There are special regulations to stop supersonic flight over populated areas.

If a sound wave reaches a large, hard, smooth object, it can bounce back to make an **echo**. Echoes can be useful, and fishermen use them to find shoals of fish. Modern fishing boats are equipped with **sonar**, an instrument which sends sound waves down into the water. If the sound waves strike a shoal of fish, the sound **reflects**, or echoes back to the instrument. This shows the direction and depth of the shoal.

Sometimes in a large hall, or theatre, sounds will bounce around the walls and ceiling. This makes it difficult to hear speech or music clearly. Curtains, carpets or special tiles known as **baffles** can be used to deaden the echoes. As a hall fills up with people, their clothes absorb sound too. Designers have to consider this when they plan how speech or music will sound inside these buildings. This science is known as **acoustics**.

Sydney opera house showing sound baffles on the ceiling. These absorb sound waves so that the audience are not aware of echoes which would blur the sound.

When an aircraft, such as Concorde, exceeds the speed of sound, a shock wave builds up at the nose of the plane, causing a sonic boom. The shock wave forms a cone behind the aircraft. A 'carpet' of sound sweeps along the ground. People on the 'carpet' hear the boom.

Frequency, pitch and loudness

SOUNDS ARE MADE by movements called **vibrations.** A vibration is a movement up and down or to and fro. Some things vibrate faster than others. For example, a mosquito beats its wings up and down six hundred times per second. We hear a high humming noise. A larger insect such as a bee may beat its wings fewer times per second so we hear a low buzzing noise.

The number of complete vibrations every second is called the **frequency.** The greater the

We can use a rubber band to make notes of different pitch. Look at the drawing. The part of the band between the pencils will vibrate when you pluck it. Hold the band half-way along with your finger and thumb and pluck again with your other hand. You will hear a higher note. This is because you have made the vibrating part of the band shorter.

Tap an empty bottle with a rod and listen to the note. Then add a little water and tap the bottle again. The note will be higher. You can

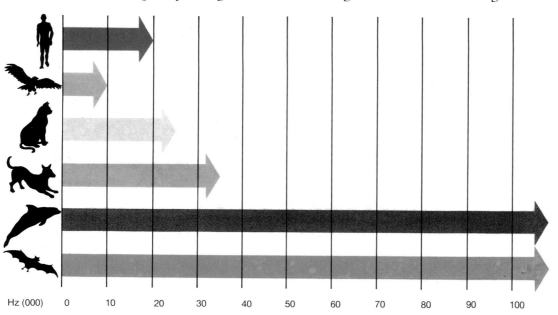

| Hz (000) | 0 | 10 | 20 | 30 | 40 | 50 | 60 | 70 | 80 | 90 | 100 |

This diagram shows the range of hearing in some animals compared with that of human beings. The human ear can hear sounds of frequencies up to 20000Hz. Higher frequencies are called ultrasonic. Bats, dolphins and some insects have hearing ranges which are ultrasonic.

frequency, the higher the sound we hear. The highness or lowness of a sound is called its **pitch.** Frequency is measured in units called **Hertz (Hz).** A Hertz equals one complete vibration per second. Most people with normal hearing can hear sounds as low as 20 Hz. A person about 18 years old may hear up to 20 000 Hz but for older people, 18 000 Hz or 16 000 Hz is the limit.

Many animals respond to human voices so we know they can hear sounds in the same frequency range to us. But some can hear higher sounds still. Cats can hear sounds up to 25 000 Hz, and dogs even higher, up to 35 000 Hz. Dogs can hear sounds from a much greater distance than human beings. People such as farmers and police who use dogs as working animals sometimes use a high frequency whistle to give orders. The dog hears the whistle but its owner only hears the rush of air.

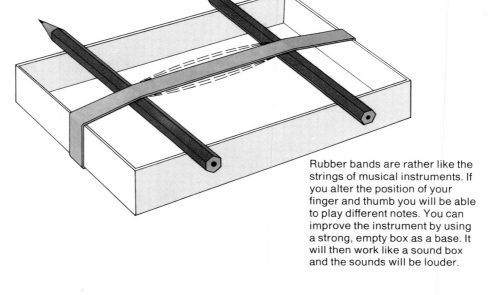

Rubber bands are rather like the strings of musical instruments. If you alter the position of your finger and thumb you will be able to play different notes. You can improve the instrument by using a strong, empty box as a base. It will then work like a sound box and the sounds will be louder.

The loudness of sounds is measured in decibels (dB). The softest sound we can hear has a value of 0dB. A jet aircraft taking off can be in the noise range of 110 to 140dB. Beyond 140dB, sound can cause pain to human ears. As a result sound levels of aircraft taking off and landing are controlled by law.

Fill eight identical bottles with carefully measured amounts of water. An octave of musical sounds can be produced by striking the bottles. You can play a tune using a wooden or metal spoon as a striker.

tune a row of similar bottles to make a scale of notes. Listen carefully as you adjust the water level in each bottle until you get just the right note.

Hold the end of a ruler flat on a table. Flick the end to make it vibrate. Now flick gently to make the vibrations smaller. You will hear a much quieter sound. Flick the ruler again to make larger vibrations. This needs more energy and you will hear a louder sound.

The size of the vibration is called the **amplitude.** The greater the amplitude the louder the sound. Loudness is measured in **decibels** (dB). Some sounds are so loud they can damage your hearing. The effect can be worse if they go on for a long time. A day at work in a noisy factory can cause ringing noises in the ears and deaden hearing for some hours afterwards. Sometimes loud sounds can cause permanent deafness.

Materials such as foam rubber and wool do not let sound pass through them easily. They absorb sound vibration well. Ear-muffs made from materials like these are often used to protect workers in noisy places. Carpets and curtains also absorb sounds. In factories false ceilings of absorbent material can be fitted. Noisy machinery can sometimes be boxed in or mounted on rubber feet to help reduce noise.

Unwanted noise is a form of pollution and many countries now have laws to prevent noise from reaching a level where it can do harm and cause discomfort.

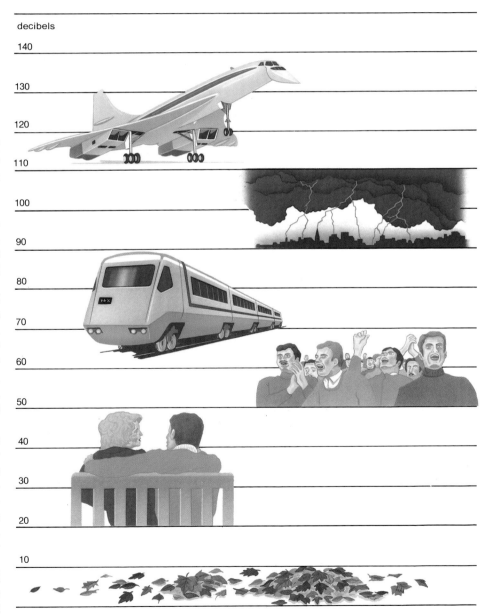

decibels

140

130

120

110

100

90

80

70

60

50

40

30

20

10

Ultrasound and echoes

RAYS OF LIGHT travel in straight lines. They can pass through transparent objects such as glass or water, but when they meet anything else they are stopped, and cast shadows. Sound does not behave in the same way. We have all heard someone shouting from the other side of a wall. Even if the other person is out of sight, the sound bends round the wall. This is called **diffraction**.

The higher the frequency of sound, the more it behaves like a beam of light. Sound which is too high for us to hear is called **ultrasound**. This can be bundled up and beamed rather like a searchlight. It will travel in a straight line without bending round objects.

Bats make use of ultrasound to detect obstacles and to find insects to eat. About two hundred years ago an Italian scientist, Lazzarro Spallanzani, covered up the eyes of some bats and discovered that they still caught as many insects as the bats without eye coverings did. How do bats find their way in the dark so skilfully? The answer was discovered by scientists this century.

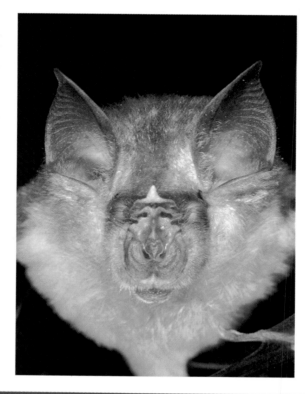

Bats are the only flying mammals and they feed on insects. They are nocturnal animals. This means that they are mainly active during night-time. The Horseshoe bat, illustrated here, has folds around the mouth shaped like a horseshoe. It sends out pulses of ultrasound through these folds.

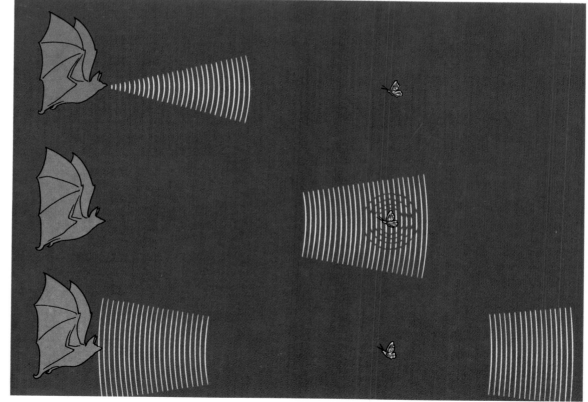

While a bat is flying it sends out high pitched squeaks, about fifty each second. These sounds cannot be heard by humans. The sound bounces back off anything solid, such as an insect or a tree. The echo is picked up by the bat's large and sensitive ears. The bat alters direction of flight to catch an insect, or to avoid a tree. Bats are superbly equipped to use ultrasound and echolocation in order to survive as nocturnal animals.

The Horseshoe bat has complicated folds of skin around its mouth and nostrils. These folds are shaped like a horseshoe, hence its unusual name. The bat uses them as a sort of horn to direct a narrow beam of ultrasound outwards in any direction. It can sweep the sound backwards and forwards to scan its surroundings.

The bat makes very short sounds about 50 to 60 milliseconds long. One millisecond is one-thousandth of a second. The frequency of the sound is between 60 and 120 kilohertz. As the bat flies nearer and nearer to an object, the sounds get faster. Young people with a wide range of hearing can sometimes just hear them. They sound like a series of clicks.

These short clicks bounce off trees or insects to make an **echo**. The bat with its large ears has very good hearing. It can hear the echoes coming back to it and these are used to judge where objects are. The longer the time between the click and the echo, the further away the object is. Bats, which are expert fliers, can swerve quickly to catch an insect every few seconds. In a laboratory test, it has been proved that they can fly through thin wires 30 cm apart without bumping into them.

It has been suggested that bats hear the flapping of insect wings, but this does not explain how they avoid the wires. Also it has been shown that bats will swerve to chase small pebbles thrown into the air. It is clear that they rely on picking up ultrasonic echoes from their prey. This is called **echolocation**.

How do bats sort out the difference between all the echoes they hear? Some will be from insects, some from trees and rocks. If we knew the answer to this question we could perhaps help blind people to find their way around more easily. Many blind people already use a kind of

echolocation. They walk along, tapping with a stick as they go. With practice, they can hear the taps echoing back from trees or other things in their path. Some blind people can use the sound of their footsteps in this way.

We have learnt that echoes can be used to find shoals of fish in the sea. Ultrasound can also be used for many purposes in industry. It can be used to open and close doors automatically, and can count the output on a production line in a factory. All that is needed is a beam of ultrasound and a **sensor**. The sensor detects if a beam is broken.

Ultrasound can also detect faults in metal. A short burst of sound is passed into the metal. Instead of passing out the other side of the metal, most of the sound bounces back as an echo. The thicker the piece of metal, the longer the time between the sound and the echo. If there is a crack in the metal the sound bounces back sooner.

Detailed knowledge of the seabed is important for people concerned with oil and mineral exploration. Echolocation is used to produce plots like this one which scientists can then study.

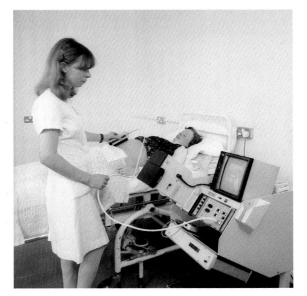

Ultrasound is sometimes used on pregnant women to make sure that the baby is developing properly. This is called monitoring, and the process is known as a scan.

Musical sounds

SOUNDS can be loud or soft, high or low, and long or short. We also find some sounds more pleasant than others because of their sound quality, or **timbre.** Musical instruments are sound machines specially designed to produce sounds for music.

Each musical instrument makes its own special type of sound. The sound depends on the

way the instrument is constructed, and on the materials used. Wood, metal or plastic each have a different effect on the sound. Earlier in the book you were told that sound waves are caused by vibrating objects. The column of air inside a wind instrument such as a trumpet vibrates when the player blows through the mouthpiece.

In a stringed instrument the string vibrates from end to end when it is plucked or bowed. If you touch a vibrating string very lightly, exactly at the centre, you will hear the note rise one **octave.** You have stopped the string vibrating from end to end, but it carries on vibrating in two halves. This produces a higher note called an overtone or **harmonic.**

The diagram below shows the range of each instrument compared with the piano keyboard and human hearing.

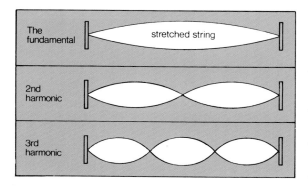

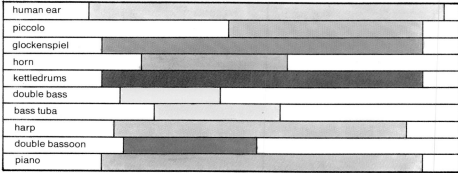

In fact, the vibration of a string is very complicated. It vibrates from end to end producing the note we call the **fundamental.** Also, at the same time, it vibrates in two, three or more parts producing many higher notes – the harmonics. The harmonics are usually much quieter than the fundamental and it takes a trained listener to pick them out.

The result is that every musical note we hear is in fact the fundamental note plus many more harmonics sounding at the same time. Some instruments produce very few harmonics, some produce very many. Also, some of the harmonics can be louder than the others. This is what gives each instrument its own unique timbre or sound quality.

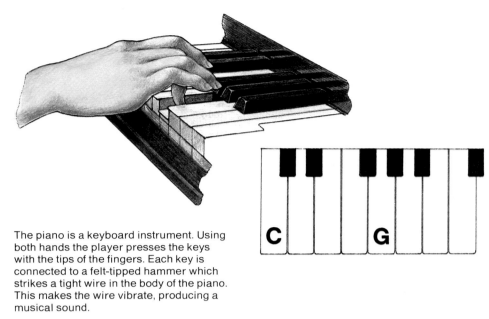

The piano is a keyboard instrument. Using both hands the player presses the keys with the tips of the fingers. Each key is connected to a felt-tipped hammer which strikes a tight wire in the body of the piano. This makes the wire vibrate, producing a musical sound.

You can prove the existence of these harmonics very easily on a piano. Play a low C loudly. The string inside the piano is producing C, the fundamental, but also a lot of harmonics as well. To hear them, hold down the G without sounding the note (press down the key very slowly) and play the low C loudly again. Take your finger off the C after a second or two. Keep your other finger on the G and listen.

You should hear the note G quite clearly even though you have not played it yourself. This is because the C string is producing the note G as one of its harmonics. The G string has picked up this harmonic and started to vibrate in sympathy with it.

The material used to make the body of the instrument also affects the timbre. Wood does not vibrate easily. This means that the tone quality is mainly due to the vibration of the string or column of air. Wood also damps or absorbs high harmonics and so most woodwind instruments sound quite pure. Brass instruments are hard and very smooth inside and so the high harmonics remain. This is why brass instruments sound bright and piercing in tone.

A player can alter the tone of an instrument by using a **mute**. In a brass instrument this is a sort of plug that is placed in the bell. In a stringed instrument the mute is a small clamp placed over the bridge. Mutes damp out many of the high harmonics and so soften the timbre. The instrument can then sound quieter and more mysterious.

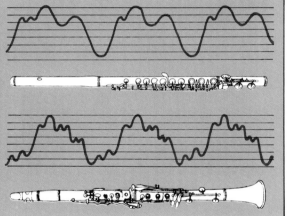

The flute *(top)* and clarinet *(bottom)* are members of the woodwind family. The waveform of the flute is rounded and smooth, because the flute has a gentle, fluid sound. The clarinet has a reedy sound, so its waveform is more jagged. In woodwinds, the sound is produced by the vibration of air inside the instrument. Notes can be made higher or lower by altering the length of the air column. This is done by covering holes with the fingers.

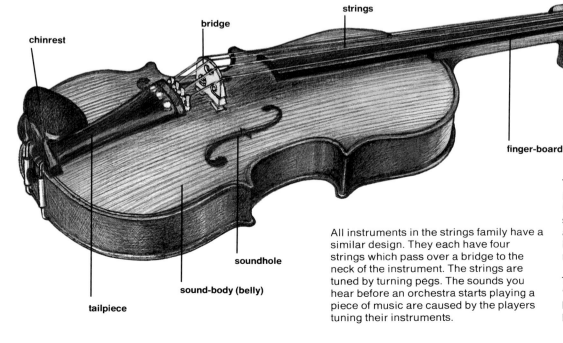

chinrest

bridge

strings

pegbox

pegs

finger-board

soundhole

sound-body (belly)

tailpiece

All instruments in the strings family have a similar design. They each have four strings which pass over a bridge to the neck of the instrument. The strings are tuned by turning pegs. The sounds you hear before an orchestra starts playing a piece of music are caused by the players tuning their instruments.

The instrument is played by holding its neck in the left hand and a bow in the right hand. The bow is moved lightly across the strings to make vibrations which we hear as musical sounds. The fingers of the left hand press the strings down making the notes lower or higher.

The violin is the smallest member of the 'strings' family of instruments. It plays the highest notes. The double bass is the largest and plays the lowest notes.

How musical instruments work

ALL MUSICAL INSTRUMENTS make sound waves. These are caused by vibrations in the instruments. For example, in a guitar the string vibrates when it is plucked. Often, musical instruments have a **resonator**, which is usually a hollow box-like part of the instrument. The resonator makes the vibrations more powerful, and as a result they sound louder.

Instruments are divided into groups according to how the musical sounds are made. Percussion instruments are struck to make the sound, and some of them, such as bells, gongs and cymbals are made of solid metal. A xylophone has wooden bars and these usually rest over a hollow box which acts as a resonator.

In Africa, **gourds** are used as resonators. These are fruits of the gourd plant which harden and become hollow when they are dried. The various types of drum are percussion instruments and these have skins stretched across a hollow resonator. Animal skins are used, but nowadays some drum-skins are made of plastic.

The important thing to remember about percussion instruments is that some of them can be tuned. That is, they can make definite notes or can even, like the xylophone, play complete tunes. The kettle-drum, or timpani, can be tuned to give notes of a definite pitch. This is done by tightening or loosening the skin of the drum by means of the screw around the rim. Instruments like this are called pitched percussion. The percussion instruments which cannot be tuned are called **unpitched**. They are used for rhythmical effects or to provide a beat like the modern drumkit.

Stringed instruments have strings stretched over a hollow box. The tighter the string is, the higher the note it makes. Thin strings also make higher notes. The shorter the length of the string, the higher the note. The player presses on the string with a finger to shorten the part of it that vibrates. This is called 'stopping' the string. On the guitar there are lines called frets to show the player where to put the finger down to make the different notes.

Percussion instruments are those which are struck with, for instance, a drumstick or mallet to give out a sound. Many of these instruments date from very early times. Some percussion instruments, such as the xylophone, can be tuned to give out a range of notes.

a gourd; **b** orchestral xylophone; **c** orchestral kettledrum; **d** wooden xylophone; **e** drumset; **f** triangle;

The guitar is one of the family of stringed instruments, but it is not played with a bow. It usually has six strings. These are plucked with the fingers of one hand. The other hand varies the notes by pressing the strings down against rides on the finger board. The banjo usually has five strings.

Woodwind instruments, as their name suggests, are wind instruments made of wood (sometimes of plastic). The player blows into a mouthpiece and this makes a column of air vibrate inside the instrument. The notes are made higher or lower when the length of the air column is altered. The player does this by opening and closing holes along the pipe. The serpent is a very old instrument. It was made from wooden sections bound together and covered in leather.

g serpent; **h** oboe; **i** double 'Pan' flute; **j** bassoon; **k** Italian bagpipe; **l** trombone; **m** French horn;

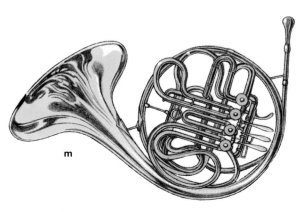

Brass instruments also contain a column of air which can be shortened or lengthened when the player presses valves. In the case of the trombone, the player uses a slide to alter the length of the air column. The notes can also be altered by changing the position of the mouthpiece against the lips.

Violins do not have frets, and you just have to learn where to place your fingers. Violins can be plucked, or the string is made to vibrate by using a bow of horsehair. In an orchestra there are four members of the violin family: violins, violas, violoncellos (cello for short) and double basses. The double bass is the biggest of the four, so it plays the lowest notes.

Wind instruments work in several different ways. They all have a tube of some sort with a column of air inside. This column of air is made to vibrate when the player blows into the mouthpiece. A flute player blows across a hole in the side of the flute. The stream of air hits the sharp edge on the far side of the hole and makes the air inside the flute vibrate.

The clarinet has a thin piece of cane called a **reed** attached to the mouthpiece, and the end of this reed is placed inside the mouth. When you blow, it vibrates, in the same way that a blade of grass can be made to vibrate when it is stretched between your thumbs.

In an oboe or bassoon, there are two pieces of cane tied together called a double-reed. This looks rather like a drinking-straw flattened at one end. You can try this yourself by taking a drinking-straw and trimming it down to about 6 cm long. Squeeze one end to flatten it. Put this end about 2 cm into your mouth and blow hard. With some practice you can make a sound.

The flute, clarinet, oboe and bassoon are all called woodwind instruments, even though some are made from metal or plastic. Brass instruments are made of metal, and the sound is caused by the vibration of the player's lips inside a cup-shaped mouthpiece. In all wind instruments the shorter the column of air, the higher the notes they make. The simplest way to get many different notes is to have several pipes of different lengths tied together.

Pan-pipes work like this. You can get the same effect with one pipe having holes cut in the side. Cover all the holes with your fingers and the lowest note is made. Uncover the holes one by one and the length of the column of air that is vibrating gets shorter and shorter. You get higher and higher notes. Woodwind instruments work in this way.

Brass instruments can make a few different notes according to how the player blows. By tightening the lips and blowing harder you can get a few higher notes called **harmonics**. To get more notes, you need some way of changing the length of the air column inside. The trombone does this easily with a **slide**. Most brass instruments use **valves** which open or close extra loops of tubing.

Signals and codes

WHEN YOU WANT to communicate with someone the simplest and quickest way is to speak to them, face to face. If the two of you are too far apart to shout, you have to send a message. One way is to write the message down. Millions of letters are sent every day through the post.

The 'marathons' people run in today are named after a battle between the Athenians and the Persians in 490 BC. The Athenians won, and the news was delivered by a messenger who ran the twenty-six miles from Marathon to Athens. However, written messages do not always reach their destination fast enough. People have always needed instant communication, especially in times of danger, either to warn others or to ask for help.

Beacon fires provide one easy way to send a message. A bonfire lit on top of a hill can be seen a long way away. Watchers on the next hill then light another fire which can be seen by the next group of watchers and so the message is passed on. When the Spanish Armada tried to invade England in 1588, a chain of beacons was lit on hills across the country. In a very short time the whole country knew what was happening. The trouble with this signal is that everyone has to known most of the message already. All the beacons could do was to show when the Spanish ships arrived. The same thing happened in 1977 to celebrate the Queen's Silver Jubilee. This time the first beacon was lit on a hill at Windsor.

The North American Indians had a better way of using fires to send messages. They produced smoke signals. Carefully timed puffs of smoke rising into the sky could be seen far away. The drumbeats of certain African tribes were used like this. Drum rhythms stand for whole words or phrases.

Another way is to use a different sign for each letter of the alphabet, and to spell out words in **code.** The Morse code is a very good example of this. Short signals (dots) and long ones (dashes) are combined in a different way for each letter.

Morse was designed to be sent along wires as electric pulses. It can also be flashed with lights or sent as bleeps of sound by radio. Most people know the international distress signal 'SOS'. If you do not you can work it out from the table.

The Morse code is named after Samuel Morse, who worked it out to use on the newly invented electric telegraph in the 1840s. This was a system of cables running from place to place. By pressing a switch the operator could send electric pulses down the wire to twitch a pointer at the other end. **Teleprinters** are now used at each end of the cable. The operator types in the message (in words) on a keyboard, and the machine does the coding. The teleprinter at the receiving end decodes the signals and prints out the words.

Language itself is a kind of code. Both the sender and the receiver of written or spoken messages have to understand the same set of symbols.

Many other codes are based on the alphabet. Before they had radios, ships could fly a set of flags from their masts to spell out words.

The Indians of North America consisted of numerous tribes. They wandered around the Great Plains in search of bison. Each tribe had its own language. Because the tribes needed to communicate with others, sign languages developed and these were understood by all. They used sign language with hand and fingers, smoke signals, trail signs and the language of feathers. There was a language for every activity.

A ·—		S ···	
B —···		T —	
C —·—·		U ··—	
D —··		V ···—	
E ·		W ·——	
F ··—·		X —··—	
G ——·		Y —·——	
H ····		Z ——··	
I ··		1 ·————	
J ·———		2 ··———	
K —·—		3 ···——	
L ·—··		4 ····—	
M ——		5 ·····	
N —·		6 —····	
O ———		7 ——···	
P ·——·		8 ———··	
Q ——·—		9 ————·	
R ·—·		0 —————	

The **Morse Code**, on the right, is a system of dots and dashes which can be sent and received in the form of electrical pulses. In the illustrations below examples are given of different ways of communicating without speech. **Semaphore** is a system of signalling by two flags held in the hand. The **Braille alphabet** is for blind people. Each letter is represented by a pattern of raised dots. In **deaf-and-dumb language** the letters of the alphabet are shown by different positions of the fingers.

The first telegraphs were huge towers with a pair of arms at the top like the hands of a clock. Each position stood for a different letter. This system is called **semaphore.** It is sometimes used by a person holding out a flag in each hand.

Blind people have a special alphabet called 'Braille'. Louis Braille, who was blind himself, invented it in 1834. A different arrangement of raised dots stands for each letter, so that books can be read by touch. Special typewriters punch the dots into the paper.

People who are deaf and dumb need a language of their own to replace speech. They use their hands to make a sign for each letter. Other hand signs stand for common words, which is quicker than spelling everything out.

The telephone system was invented in 1875 by Alexander Graham Bell. The electric signals running along the cables reproduce the vibrations made by the sound of your voice in the mouthpiece. The great advantage of the telephone is that anyone can use it. You do not need a special code to send an instant message – except the telephone number of the person you want to speak to.

Through the ages people from different continents have developed ways of sending messages. The great tradition of African drum language has been overtaken by modern methods. In its day it was a fast and efficient way of passing information from one tribe to another.

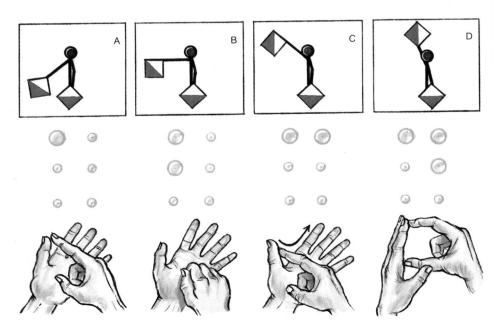

Electronics

THE NINETEENTH CENTURY was a time of great inventions, many of which helped us to make important steps forward in communicating with one another. Some inventions were possible only because of earlier ones. Among the more important were the electric light, telegraph, and telephone. Some of these would not have been possible but for electricity. This is something we all take for granted today, but let us look at what it is.

All matter is made up of atoms. Each atom has a central **nucleus** with a positive charge, and a number of **electrons** moving rapidly about it. The electrons have a negative charge. In some materials, particularly metals, there are large numbers of free electrons. This means that some electrons are not bound to single atoms, but move freely about the metal. The free electrons move in all directions, at speeds of several hundreds of metres per second.

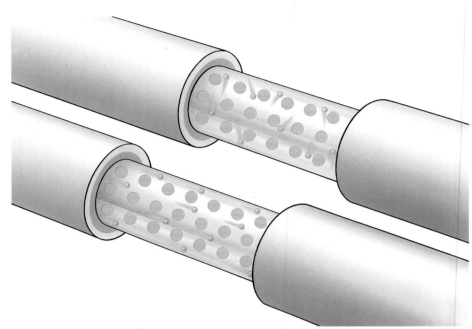

The top diagram shows atoms and free electrons in a metal conductor. The free electrons are moving randomly, that is to say in any direction. When the conductor is connected across a battery the free electrons move in one direction as shown in the lower diagram.

Sir John Ambrose Fleming, 1849–1945. He invented the diode rectifier which allows electrical current to flow easily in one direction.

If a wire or a piece of metal is connected across a battery, one end of it becomes electrically positive and the other negative. Since electrons have a negative charge, they are attracted to the positive end of the metal. Only free electrons are able to move through the metal; many stay bound to the atoms. The movement of the free electrons is not constant. They hit other atoms all the time and are moved from the direction in which they are trying to go. This is called electrical **resistance.** When the electrons collide with other atoms, some heat is produced. The collisions make the metal hotter. The free electrons tend to move towards the positive end of the metal. This movement is called an **electric current.** The higher the electric current, the more heat is produced, and the hotter the metal gets.

Electronics is the name given to the science which describes the movement of the free electrons, and how we control this. There are many ways in which we use electronics. Some examples are radio, radar, cathode-ray tubes, tape recorders and television. We call all of these pieces of electronic equipment. Nowadays, we are very used to having electronic equipment as part of our lives, but where did it all begin?

If we have a stream of water flowing in a pipe, we control it by using something called a **valve**. The kitchen tap in your home is a kind of valve. Open or close it, and you can vary the amount of water coming out. Doing the same thing with electricity is more complicated. In 1904, Professor Ambrose Fleming invented the **diode rectifier**, which only allowed electricity to flow easily in one direction. Shortly afterwards, in 1907, an American, Lee De Forest, made a **triode** valve, which was the first device which could actually control the flow of electricity.

Electronic valves are very delicate because they are made of glass, like an electric light bulb. A valve is only able to control electricity if all the air has been removed from inside it. This is called a **vacuum.** A triode valve has three main parts, known as **electrodes.** The first, called the **cathode**, is heated to give off a cloud of electrons. The second, called the **anode**, is situated at the opposite end of the valve from the cathode, and collects the electrons. Between the anode and cathode is a wire grid with open spaces. The grid controls the flow of electrons from the cathode to the anode. The anode is made strongly positive compared with the cathode. This makes the negatively charged electrons flow more easily. The grid is nearer the cathode than the anode, and is made slightly more negative than the cathode. By varying how negative the grid is compared with the cathode, the electric current (the number of electrons) flowing across the valve may be controlled.

This is very important because it enables the triode valve to be used as an **amplifier.** In other words, it may be used to turn a small electrical signal into a larger one. Another important discovery was that several valves together could act as a switch. This is a device which may be either 'closed', allowing an electric current to flow, or 'open', preventing the flow of a current.

Valves quickly became used in all kinds of electrical equipment, but there were problems. They were easily broken and needed large amounts of electricity to make them work. They also became very hot and needed fans to blow cool air over them. Equipment containing valves was therefore difficult to move and keep in working order. Because of these disadvantages, modern electronic equipment does not use valves. Instead, **transistors** are used. Here, the free electrons move inside solid matter, instead of in a vacuum as is the case with the valves.

This picture shows the thousand millionth valve produced by the Mullard plant at Blackburn, England, in forty years of manufacturing.

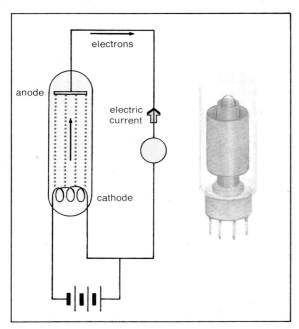

A diode is a valve with two electrodes, inside a glass bulb from which air has been removed. The negative electrode, the cathode, gives off a stream of electrons when heated. These are attracted to the positive electrode, a metal plate called the anode. Since the anode cannot give out electrons, current can only flow in one direction. Alternating current (AC) which changes from one direction to another, when applied, is rectified or converted to direct current (DC).

The triode, developed by Lee de Forest, has a third electrode, called a grid, between the anode and the cathode. This is given a negative charge which boosts the flow of electrons between cathode and anode. If the charge on the grid is varied the triode can be used as an amplifier.

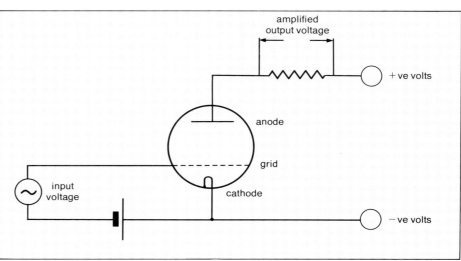

Semiconductors

THE IMPORTANT DISCOVERY of the transistor was made on 23rd December 1947 by Walter Brattain, William Shockley, and John Bardeen of the Bell Telephone Laboratories, USA. They found that the flow of electricity could be controlled with a small device, which needed neither heat nor a vacuum to make it work.

We have already seen how metals, which have plenty of free electrons, will allow an electric current to flow. Substances like this are called **conductors**. However, some materials have no free electrons and they do not allow an electric current to pass through them. These are called **insulators**. **Semiconductors** are a special type of solid material which are in between a conductor and an insulator.

Imagine a line of cars held up at a level crossing. There is a space between the gate and the first car. When the gate opens the first car moves forward and the space moves backward. This goes on down the line. The cars (electrons) move in one direction and the spaces (holes) move in the other direction.

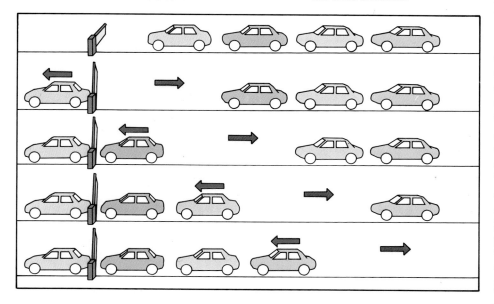

At very low temperatures, every electron in a semiconductor is tightly bound to the nucleus of its atom. At room temperature, some of the electrons may break free from their atoms, and become free electrons. When a negatively charged electron moves away from its atom, it leaves behind a vacancy. We call this vacancy a **hole.** Since this atom will now have a positive charge as a result of losing the electron, an electron from a neighbouring atom may be attracted to it. The hole in the first atom will then be filled, but another will appear in the nearby atom, whose electron has just moved. It is as though the hole has moved from one atom to another.

After doping, there are extra electrons (blue) in the n-type semiconductor material. There are extra holes (red) in the p-type material.

Under normal conditions, the movement of holes through a semiconductor is quite random. However, if a piece of semiconductor is connected across a battery, one end of it becomes positive and the other negative. The negative free electrons will be attracted towards the positive end, and they will tend to move in one direction filling the holes in nearby atoms as they do so. It then appears that the holes are moving in the other direction towards the negative end of the semiconductor. The holes move as if they were particles with a positive charge. The current is also carried by the free electrons present. These are equal in number to the holes in a pure semiconductor, and drift in the opposite direction. The electron-hole pairs are called **charge carriers.**

If a very small amount of another substance (one part in a million) is added to a semiconductor, the number of charge carriers present may be greatly increased. This process is called **doping** the semiconductor. The number of holes or electrons may be changed so that they are no longer equal in number. If a small amount of phosphorus, arsenic or antimony is added to a semiconductor, an enormous increase occurs in the number of electron carriers. The material is then called an **n-type semiconductor.** The letter 'n' stands for the negative charge on the electron. If a little boron or indium is added to a semiconductor, an enormous increase occurs in the number of holes. This material is called a **p-type semiconductor.** The letter 'p' stands for the positive charge on a hole.

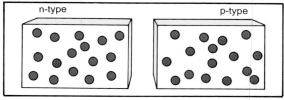

In an n-type material the negatively charged electrons are attracted by the positive battery terminal. In a p-type material the positive holes are attracted towards the negative terminal.

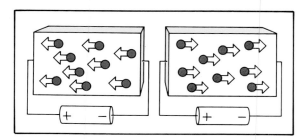

By a special process, pieces of 'p' and 'n' type semiconductor may be melted so that the two pieces are joined together. Where the two pieces join is called a **p-n junction**. This lets electricity flow easily in one direction only. It is a diode rectifier, or junction diode. Although the junction diode is useful, the transistor is even more so, because, just like the triode valve, it may be used both as a switch and as an amplifier.

The transistor is made from three layers of 'p' and 'n' type semiconductor. The three layers are called the **emitter**, the **base** and the **collector**. Transistors come in two types. In the p-n-p transistor, the emitter is p-type, the base is n-type and the collector p-type. In an n-p-n transistor, the emitter is n-type, the base is p-type and the collector is n-type. The base is a much thinner layer of semiconductor than the other two. The three layers of a transistor correspond to the three electrodes of the triode valve. The base corresponds to the grid of the valve and the other two layers to the cathode and anode. In an n-p-n transistor, the collector must be made more positive than the emitter. The reverse is true for the p-n-p transistor.

The earliest transistors were made of germanium, but nowadays **silicon** is almost always used. Silicon is cheap and widely available. Because of their tiny size and the small amount of electricity they consume, transistors completely changed the design of communications equipment. Modern electronic devices no longer use many single transistors. Instead, large numbers of electronic components are combined on to a single thin wafer of silicon about five millimetres square. This is called an **integrated circuit**. Modern integrated circuits may contain over one million components on a single silicon wafer. Although the number of components is very large, they consume only a tiny amount of electricity, and little heat is given out. The thin piece of silicon with the components on it is sometimes called a 'silicon chip'.

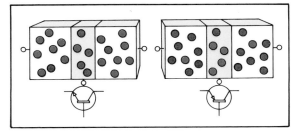
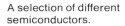

A transistor is made of a sandwich of different types of semiconductors, either n-p-n *(far left)* or p-n-p *(left)*. They work in much the same way as valves used to, but are smaller, lighter and use much less power. Their invention has led to the modern compact electronic equipment that we now take for granted.

A selection of different semiconductors.

A silicon chip compared in size with a strawberry.

How the telephone works

THE NAME we give to the sending of messages over a distance is telecommunication. The messages are sent from something called the **transmitter**, and at the other end are picked up by the **receiver.** So that a message may be sent from transmitter to receiver, it first has to be changed into electrical signals. In the telegraph this was done by the Morse tapping key. In the telephone and on radio it is done by a **microphone**; and in television by a TV camera.

Once the message has been turned into an electrical signal, it is then added to a high frequency radio wave. This can transmit it most easily. The radio wave is called a **carrier wave** because it carries the electrical signals (our message) from the transmitter to the receiver. In radio or television, the carrier wave is usually sent through the air. The process of adding electrical signals on to a carrier wave is called **modulation.** It is possible to send many different frequencies of carrier wave along cables or through the air at the same time. This is called **multiplexing.** It is very important, because it makes it possible to send several thousand two-way telephone calls along one cable at the same time.

At the receiving end of any telecommunication system, special electronic circuits sort out the electrical signals which are our message, from the carrier wave. These signals are then amplified and sent to the receiver. This

How a long distance telephone call is routed.

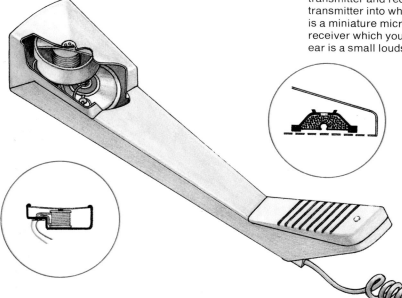

A telephone handset combines transmitter and receiver. The transmitter into which you speak is a miniature microphone. The receiver which you hold to your ear is a small loudspeaker.

might be your telephone handset, a transistor radio or a television screen.

The handset of the telephone has both a transmitter in the mouthpiece, and a receiver in the earpiece. The mouthpiece contains a carbon microphone. This has a thin sheet or **diaphragm** at the front which is in contact with a number of lightly packed carbon grains. As you speak into the microphone, your voice vibrates the diaphragm. This packs the carbon grains more tightly, or less tightly together. When the grains are closer together, an electrical current passes through them more easily. When the grains are more loosely packed, the current does not pass through so easily. As you speak, the diaphragm moves. This in turn causes the grains to move and thus produces a varying electrical current related to the voice signals. These electrical signals may then be added to a carrier wave and sent along a cable.

At the receiving end of the telephone line, the electrical signals are sorted out from the carrier wave, and enter the earpiece of the person you are calling. Here the electrical signals are turned into sound waves again. These sound waves are heard by your ear. They are an exact copy of the sounds spoken into the mouthpiece at the other end of the line.

To contact another telephone number, you first pick up the handset from its cradle. As the cradle rises, a switch closes and makes an electrical connection between your telephone and the telephone exchange. This is a building full of electronic circuits, to which all the telephone lines in your area are connected. It is the job of the exchange to connect telephones to one another. But how does the exchange know who you want to call? First you must dial the number.

When you dial a number the circular dial plate rotates a set of cogs inside the telephone. These open and close a pair of electrical contacts. As you dial each figure, the contacts open and close and produce a number of electrical **pulses.** In the modern push-button phone, an electronic circuit remembers the sequence of pulses produced and then sends them, one after the other to the exchange. When the electronic circuits in the exchange receive the pulses, they operate a series of switches which link your tele-

A modern telephone exchange. More and more exchanges are now automatic in operation. New types of switches, using transistors, are gradually replacing the mechanical systems still used in many parts of the world.

A modern push-button telephone set. The caller can key in the number required faster than with a dialling system.

phone with that of the person you are calling. Sometimes this may mean that the line is connected through several different exchanges. Modern telephone exchanges use integrated circuits to switch the telephone lines. This means that they make faster, more silent and more reliable connections. Electronic telephone exchanges can handle many thousands of calls at the same time. Most exchanges are completely automatic, even for international calls from one country to another.

Most telephone cables are put under the ground. Many have been laid beneath the oceans of the world to connect continents. The cables are usually made of copper or alum-

inium. These metals are becoming more difficult to obtain, and more expensive. Telephone engineers believe that in the future, cables will be replaced by bundles of **fibre optics.**

A fibre optic is a very thin tube of silica glass. Its diameter is between thirty and one hundred millionths of a metre. This is similar to the thickness of a human hair. With a cable made of fibre optics, telephone messages would no longer be changed into varying electrical signals. Instead, they would use a light source of changing brightness. This varying beam of light would pass along the fibre optic at 300 000 kilometres per second. Not only is this extremely fast, but the light beam is not affected by the electrical noise which may spoil the normal telephone conversation. Fibre optics will greatly reduce the number of cables needed for very complicated telecommunication systems.

Satellites orbiting above the Earth are being used more and more for long distance telephone communications.

Fibre optic cable is now used in telephone lines between cities. It may soon replace the solid copper link to the home itself. When this happens we will have as many communication channels as we want.

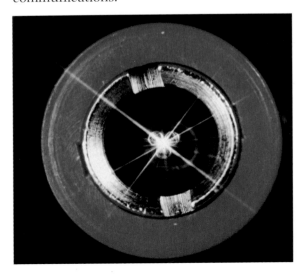

41

The microphone and tape recording

TAPE RECORDING was first thought of in about 1898, but it was not until the Second World War that the technique was fully developed.

Sounds which we hear are produced by air molecules moving rapidly backwards and forwards. To record sound, the changes in air pressure must be converted into varying electrical currents. The thing which does this is called a **microphone.**

There are many different types of microphone but they all contain a **diaphragm**. This is a thin disk of metal or sometimes plastic which can move backwards and forwards when the moving air hits it.

As we have seen, the telephone mouthpiece uses a carbon microphone. The diaphragm is made of **graphite** (a type of carbon). A second fixed disk of graphite forms a 'sandwich'. The 'filling' is made of small carbon grains loosely packed between the disks. As the diaphragm vibrates it squashes and releases the carbon grains. These have the property that when they are squeezed the **electrical resistance** changes. When a battery is connected across the microphone the electrical current gets stronger or weaker as the pressure on the grains from the voice vibrations varies.

Another type is the **moving-coil microphone.** This is the type most widely used today. Here the diaphragm is fixed to a small, light coil of wire. This coil can move between the poles of a tiny magnet. An important discovery was made in the nineteenth century which showed that if

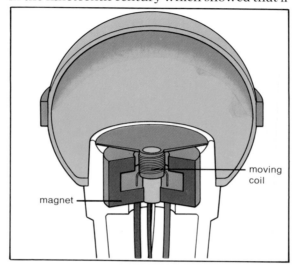

There are a number of different types of microphone. The moving-coil microphone is widely used. Sound waves strike the diaphragm which vibrates. The diaphragm is fixed to a coil of wire which moves between the poles of an **electromagnet**. As it moves the current changes with the rhythm of the vibrating diaphragm.

The recording head on a tape recorder is a small electromagnet with a gap facing the tape. As the varying sound signals reach the coil of wire surrounding the electromagnet, the magnetic field in the gap also varies. The unrecorded tape, with its tiny crystal magnets in a jumble, moves past the recording head. The varying magnetic field in the gap re-arranges the tiny crystals into a pattern. In this way the sound signals are stored on the tape.

When the tape is re-wound and played back again, the pattern of tiny magnets on the tape sets up electrical signals in the coil of the playback head. The signals are amplified and wired to the speaker.

In the enlarged illustration iron oxide crystals are seen passing the recording head. They are arranged in a fixed pattern on the magnetic tape.

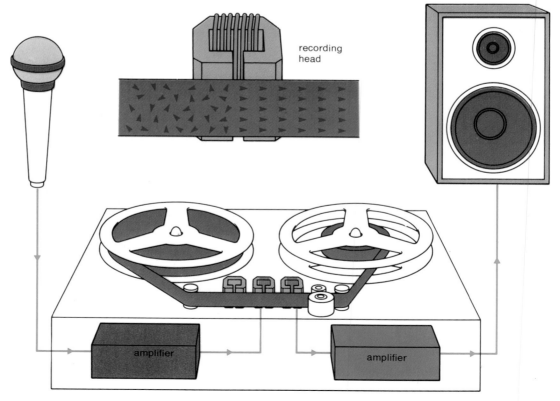

a wire moves near the end of a magnet, an electric current is produced. This current flows in the coil of the microphone and changes with the rhythm of the moving diaphragm.

In whichever way the electric currents are made, they need to be made bigger by an **amplifier.** These changing currents represent the original sounds. They can be stored for the future on **magnetic recording tape** using a **recording head.**

Magnetic recording tape is made of a very thin ribbon of plastic. It is coated on one side with a layer of powdered iron oxide, making that side look dull. Through a microscope iron oxide is seen to be made up of many thin, needle-like crystals. A device called a recording head is used to move these crystals around into different positions on the tape. The movement is the same as when a magnet is brought close to a magnetic compass. The compass needle will swing round and then point in a certain direction.

The recording head is a small ring of metal, usually iron, with a tiny gap cut in one side. A coil of wire is wrapped around the ring. When an electric current is passed through the coil, an **electromagnet** is formed. The gap is there so that some of this magnetism can 'leak out' of the ring. As the tape slowly passes the recording head, the magnetism caused by the electric currents moves the iron oxide crystals around into a pattern which represents the original sound. The pattern will stay fixed on the tape until we want to erase it. Erasing can be thought of as jumbling up the crystals on the tape.

To play back a recording, the tape is moved past the same head as was used to record it. The iron oxide crystals now act as tiny magnets causing very small electric currents to pass through the coil of the head. Since the same head is used for both jobs, it is often called a **record/playback head.** The electric currents are then amplified. Usually this is done by the same amplifier as when recording. The larger currents go to a **loudspeaker** or **headphones.** These work in the opposite way to moving-coil microphones. The currents pass through a coil of wire which is very close to a strong magnet, causing the coil to move. The coil is fixed to a diaphragm and so this also moves. The diaphragm causes the air to vibrate and we hear these vibrations as sound.

By the mid-1960s magnetic tape was being made thinner and narrower. This meant that recordings could be made on much smaller tapes. The tape was then enclosed in a plastic case and the **cassette** was produced. Tape recorders could then be made much smaller and more portable. Some modern tape machines are hardly bigger than the cassette itself.

The Sony Walkman is a tiny cassette tape player which has sound coming through headphones only. It is so small that walkers and workers can wear it without any difficulty.

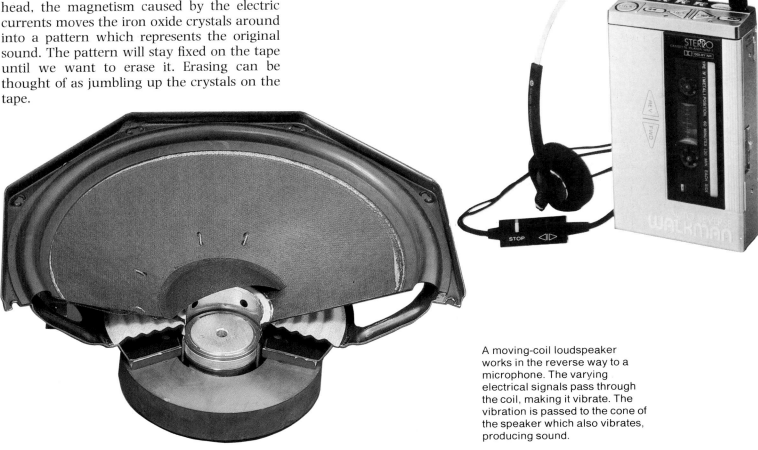

A moving-coil loudspeaker works in the reverse way to a microphone. The varying electrical signals pass through the coil, making it vibrate. The vibration is passed to the cone of the speaker which also vibrates, producing sound.

Radio waves and the ionosphere

RADIO WAVES are one type of **electromagnetic wave** which travel through the air or a vacuum. They spread out from the source in much the same way as ripples move across water when a stone is dropped into a pond. The person who first discovered these waves in 1864 and began to think of uses for them was the Scottish mathematician, James Clerk Maxwell.

In 1884, the German physicist Heinrich Rudolph Hertz found out much more about these waves. He discovered that they behave in a similar way to light (which is also a type of electromagnetic wave). They move in straight lines. They can be reflected (as light can be in a mirror) and they travel very fast at about 300 000 000 metres per second. In fact he did so much work on these waves that they are sometimes known as **Hertzian waves.** The number of wave movements passing a given point in one second is known as the **frequency,** and the unit of measurement is the Hertz.

The first ever use of radio waves probably took place in 1882 when signals were sent from

James Clerk Maxwell, 1831–79 *(right)*. He was the first scientist to realise that light and other waves are electromagnetic.

Heinrich Rudolf Hertz, 1857–94 *(left)*. He proved the existence of electromagnetic waves

the Isle of Wight to the south coast of England. However, the most famous person working on radio transmission must be the Italian engineer, Guglielmo Marconi. He moved to England to carry out much of his work, and by 1898 he had set up a radio station on the south coast for communicating with ships. In 1901 he carried out the famous experiment where he sent the first ever signals from Poldhu in Cornwall across the Atlantic Ocean to Newfoundland in Canada. In these early experiments a series of **pulses** was sent. The radio wave was switched on and off to send a sort of code, rather like Morse code.

There is a wide range of radio waves all with different frequencies. This range is split up into sections. The different sections or **bands** are used for different purposes. The best known bands are those used for domestic radio, for example, BBC Radio 4. These are known as the long- and medium-wave bands. The next section with a higher frequency is known as the short-wave band. This is used for very long distance communication. Using this band, signals can travel right round the world. There are other regions with even higher frequencies. These are the **VHF** (very high frequency) and **UHF** (ultra high frequency) bands. VHF has a short range and is used for local radio stations and by the police, fire and ambulance services. UHF is used mainly for television signals and radar.

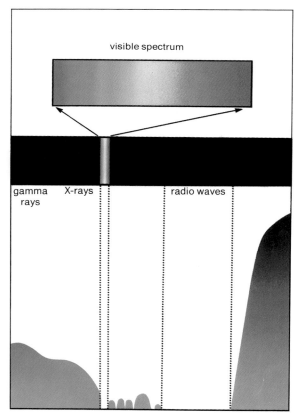

visible spectrum

gamma rays   X-rays   radio waves

Electromagnetic waves spread out through space in all directions. Light is only a small part of the complete spectrum. Radio waves have a lower frequency than light, X-rays and gamma rays have a higher frequency.

The distance that radio waves travel round the Earth depends upon the **ionosphere.** This is a part of the Earth's atmosphere which extends from about 60 km to about 500 km above the Earth's surface. It is made up of gas particles which are electrically charged. These particles are known as **ions,** hence the name ionosphere. The ions are produced by **ultraviolet** rays from the Sun hitting the gas particles. The ionosphere can act like a mirror and reflect many radio waves.

Two English scientists, Oliver Heaviside and Sir Edward Victor Appleton discovered that there are two distinct layers in the ionosphere.

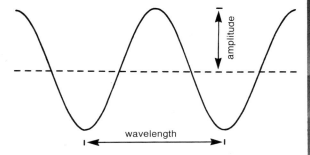

Wavelength is the distance between two peaks or troughs. Amplitude is the height of the wave. The shorter the wavelength, the higher is the frequency.

Long wave

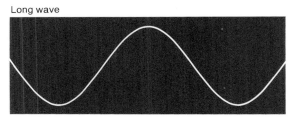

VHF

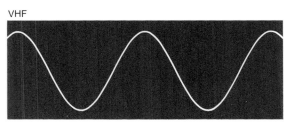

UHF

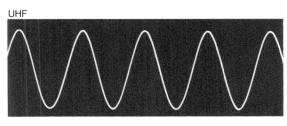

Radio waves vary in frequency, from long wave, low frequency, to the VHF and UHF short wave bands. All waves travel at the same speed.

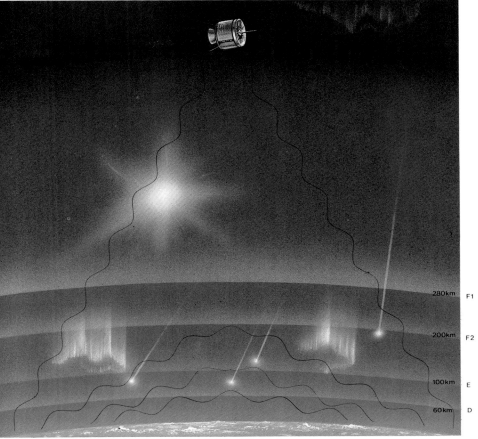

280km F1

200km F2

100km E

60km D

VHF and UHF waves pass through the ionosphere and can be bounced back to Earth by communication satellites. Long and medium waves are reflected from the D and E layers, short waves from the F layers.

The lower region, from about 60 km above the Earth, is known as the Heaviside layer or sometimes as the 'E' layer. This part of the ionosphere reflects the long-wave and medium-wave radio signals. As can be seen in the diagram, this means that a radio wave can 'bounce' between the Earth and the E layer. It can travel quite some distance round the Earth this way.

Unfortunately, each time the wave reflects from the ionosphere, some of the strength of the signal is lost. This means that eventually the signal will be too weak to be heard.

The upper region, extending from about 150 km to about 500 km above the Earth, is known as the Appleton or 'F' layer. This tends to reflect the short-wave band. As this layer is much higher, the radio waves do not have to be reflected so many times to go a long distance. The signal can still be heard a long way away.

VHF and UHF signals are not reflected by the ionosphere. In fact they pass straight through it. This means that these bands can only be used for short-range communication. The fact that UHF goes through the ionosphere can be useful, for it is this band which is used for communication with satellites and spacecraft.

How radio works

RADIO WAVES are of such a high frequency that we cannot hear them. Fortunately radio receivers can be made which are able to detect these waves. A radio wave on its own does not tell us anything apart from the fact that a wave is there. A method must be found to add information on to the basic wave. This is called **modulation.**

The simplest form of modulation is to switch the wave on and off in some form of code. This is the way Marconi sent the first signals across the Atlantic Ocean. He used a device which produced sparks in a set pattern. A spark is an electromagnetic wave which only lasts for a very short time. You can see that this is true by the following experiment.

An electric motor produces a lot of sparks. If you listen to a radio set with the motor of, for example, a vacuum cleaner running close by, you will hear a crackling noise on the radio. The vacuum cleaner is working like Marconi's early transmitter. A spark is not just one electromagnetic wave but millions of them, each having a different frequency. You can prove this by watching the television while doing the previous experiment. Flecks of white will be seen on the screen because you are picking up the vacuum cleaner's transmission on UHF also. If we still used a spark transmitter today, there could only be one radio station broadcasting at any one time. An English physicist, Sir Oliver Lodge, realised that this was a problem and invented a device which could reduce the number of frequencies needed for each signal.

The basic radio wave which carries the information is known as the **carrier wave.** Modern transmitters tend to use one of two possible methods of modulation. The first is **amplitude modulation,** or AM for short. Here the size of the carrier wave is changed in step with the changing electrical currents produced by a microphone. In the second method, **frequency modulation** (FM), the frequency of the carrier is changed in step with the microphone's current. Using AM or FM it is possible to send not just codes but speech and music as well. These are called audio signals.

In order to transmit radio programmes, electric currents from the microphone are first amplified. The carrier wave is produced and the two waves (audio and carrier) are added together in a 'mixer'. The combined signals are amplified again and passed on to the aerial of the broadcasting station where they spread out into the air as electromagnetic waves.

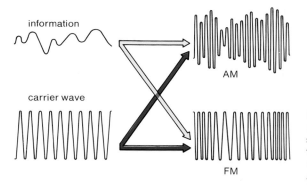

Sir Oliver Lodge, 1851–1940.

Radio stations transmit an unmodulated carrier wave. The sounds which are to be transmitted alter, that is to say, modulate, the carrier wave in amplitude (AM) or frequency (FM).

Marconi, in 1901, with transmitting and receiving apparatus similar to that used for sending and receiving the first wireless signal across the Atlantic.

The electromagnetic waves travel to the aerial in the receiver. Different types of aerial are used for receiving different frequency signals. A small coil of wire is usually used for long wave and medium wave signals. A long length of wire is used for the short wave band and a short metal rod for the VHF and UHF bands. In each case, as the electromagnetic wave passes by the coil, wire or rod, tiny electrical currents are produced in the aerial.

As the aerial picks up many different radio stations at the same time, we must now pick out the one we need. To do this a **tuned circuit** is used. This is made up of a small coil of wire and a **capacitor.** The value of one of these, usually the capacitor, can be varied. This is done by turning the tuning control on the radio receiver. At this stage the signals are still very small and so have to be amplified. The next step is to remove the carrier wave. It has done its job in carrying the information from the transmitter and is no longer needed. This is the opposite to modulation and is called **demodulation.** We now have the audio signals left but they are still very small. They have to be amplified again and are finally fed to a loudspeaker.

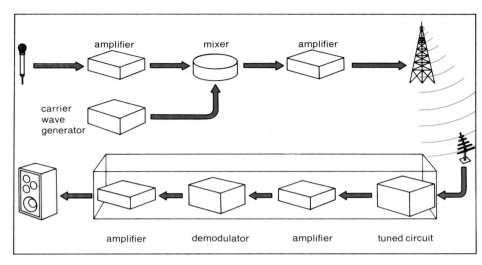

There are more uses for radio than just domestic entertainment programmes. The police, fire, ambulance and coastguard services use short range VHF radio links between their base stations and mobiles (cars or ships). It is even possible to talk to nearby friends using citizen band (CB) radio. If you look around, you are sure to spot long CB aerials fixed to cars and house roofs.

This diagram shows the steps which take place between transmission of a radio programme and its reception in the loudspeaker.

American policeman with two-way radio.

Modern portable radio.

Sending pictures over a distance

In order for a picture to be sent over a distance, it has to be sent as an electrical signal. This can be done only if the scene is broken down into many parts. The many parts must then be put together again after the electrical signal has been sent so that the person at the receiving end can see the complete picture.

Sending a picture over a distance is not the same as sending sounds such as a piece of music. Music is a series of notes, produced one after the other. If each note is changed into an electrical signal, the receiver can change these back again into a series of notes. The notes will follow each other in exactly the same order as when they were sent.

However, a picture is not like this. All the small pieces of information which make up the picture are received by the camera at the same time. To change each detail into an electrical signal and send them all at once is not possible. What we need to do is to send the information in the picture as a series of signals, one after the

The moving pictures which we see on television screens are sent out and received as electrical signals. These signals are transmitted over great distances by tall aerials. They are received by aerials placed as high as possible on individual homes.

other. We must do this in such a way that the person at the other end can then remake the original picture.

Imagine you have a jigsaw puzzle of one thousand pieces. If someone dipped into the box and handed you one piece at a time in any order, it would be very difficult for you to make up the picture. However, suppose someone had the completed jigsaw in front of them. They could then hand you one piece at a time, starting with the top row, moving from left to right, then the second row and so on. It would be an easy matter for you to put the jigsaw together again. This is the way in which a television picture is broken down into small parts and put back again by the receiver. It is called electronic **scanning**.

Many people believe that the Scotsman, John Logie Baird, was the inventor of television. In fact, as early as 1923 a Russian American named Vladimir Zworykin demonstrated a television system. His work was important because the system was electronic. His **iconoscope** was the first real electronic television camera. He used a **cathode-ray** tube as a receiver.

By contrast, Baird's crude apparatus was mechanical. He used a rotating scanning disk

A typical television camera.

In order to transmit pictures a process known as scanning is used. The television camera scans the scene from left to right and line by line, completing twenty-five complete pictures in one second. Each picture varies slightly from the previous one and this is the way movement is recorded. As the scene is scanned the variations of lightness and darkness are converted into varying electrical signals.

pierced with holes. Baird saw no future in an electronic system. Sadly, though Baird was the first to show that television was possible, his 'machine' was never widely used. In 1934, the BBC decided to use an electronic system, built by Marconi-EMI, much to Baird's disappointment.

In a television camera the scene is scanned in much the same way as you read a page of this book. The scene is scanned one line at a time, from left to right. When each line is completed, a new line is started, until the bottom of the picture is reached. Then a new picture is started, just as you start a new page. The picture is divided into a large number of small, equal-sized parts. These are known as picture elements, or **pixels**.

In the TV camera, the picture which we need to televise is focused on to a special screen. This screen is coated with a material which allows an electric charge to build up on its surface according to how much light falls on it. Each pixel is scanned by an electron beam, so that the amount of charge at that point on the screen is changed into an electrical signal. This varies according to the amount of light falling on the pixel which is being scanned.

A modern TV set can be used to receive general information in the form of words and images. The process is known as teletext. It includes such things as weather forecasts and travel information.

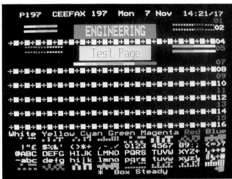

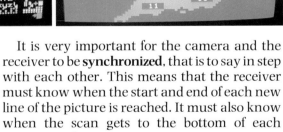

The picture seen on a television screen close-to. The picture is made up of a large number of parallel lines. Each line varies in brightness from end to end. In each second twenty-five complete scans are made from top to bottom. Put another way, any point on a scene is scanned twenty-five times in one second.

It is very important for the camera and the receiver to be **synchronized**, that is to say in step with each other. This means that the receiver must know when the start and end of each new line of the picture is reached. It must also know when the scan gets to the bottom of each picture, so that it can start a new one.

The rate at which pictures are scanned by the camera, and at which they are shown on the screen is very important. If less than fifteen pictures were sent to the television screen each second, it would flicker. In most countries a rate of twenty-five per second is used. Each picture is completed in two stages. In the first scan, the electron beam making up the picture in the receiver scans only the odd numbered lines. The beam then goes back to the top of the picture and scans the even numbered lines. This happens too fast for your eyes to detect it. In most countries the TV system uses 625 lines to make up each picture. In USA the standard is 405 lines.

Colour television

How are radio waves used to send and receive television pictures? We must first look at black and white television which is simpler. Light from the scene being televised is focused by the camera lens on to a special screen. This screen lies inside a tube from which all the air has been removed. This is called a vacuum tube.

The screen on which the light falls has a thin coat of material which is sensitive to light. This is said to be **photosensitive**. An electric charge builds up on the layer, depending upon how much light falls on each part of it. The more light there is, the more charge builds up. At the far end of the vacuum tube, away from the screen, there is an electron gun. This fires a beam of electrons at the screen. The beam is controlled so that it scans the photosensitive layer from side to side, moving from top to bottom.

At any movement, the photosensitive screen carries an exact copy of the view seen by the camera, as an amount of electric charge. The bright parts of the picture will have large amounts of charge on the screen, and the dark parts only a small charge. The beam scans the layer line by line. As it passes over each position in the layer, the amount of charge is changed into a varying signal. The job of the camera is to view the picture as a pattern of light and dark picture elements (**pixels**). It then breaks down the pattern into a series of closely spaced, horizontal lines. Finally, it produces varying electric signals from the light and dark shades in each layer.

The line by line signals are then transmitted with scanning pulses in step with the signals. These mark the beginning and end of each line of the picture. The signals which contain the picture are combined with other signals produced by the sound which goes with the picture. All these signals are then put on to an ultra-high frequency (UHF) radio wave, known as the UHF **carrier wave**.

The TV aerial picks up the carrier wave. It then sorts out the signals which relate to the light and dark pixels and the sound. The picture brightness and the **synchronizing** signals are fed to a **cathode-ray tube** (CRT). The front end of this is the TV screen you look at. An electron gun at the back of the CRT produces a beam of electrons. The synchronizing (timing) pulses are fed to wire coils around the tube of the CRT.

These make the electron beam scan backwards and forwards in step with the scans of the TV camera. The brightness signals are fed to the **anode** of the CRT. They cause the speed of the electrons in the beam to change. The faster the beam travels, the brighter the spot it makes on the coated screen of the CRT. The coating on the screen is made of materials which are known as **phosphors**. These glow when electrons hit them. In this way, we see a light and dark picture on the screen which matches the one produced inside the TV camea.

Colour television works in a similar way. The way the colour is produced is interesting. Any colour can be made up by mixing light of the three primary colours, blue, green and red, in different amounts.

In the colour TV camera, a system of glass **prisms**, mirrors and colour filters breaks up the image formed by the camera lens into these three colours. Each of these three coloured images is then scanned by one of three separate electron beams in three vacuum tubes. These change the blue, green and red colours in the original picture into three different signals.

The three colour signals, plus the synchronization pulses are transmitted. As soon as these are received by the aerial of the colour TV set,

A black-and-white TV camera converts a moving scene into varying electrical signals, so that they can be transmitted by radio waves. Light passes through the lens and falls on a plate which is sensitive to light. The electric charge on the plate varies according to the brightness of the image. The more light there is, the greater the charge. An electron 'gun' scans the plate with a stream of electrons. The electrons are reflected at varying strengths and converted into electrical signals which can be transmitted.

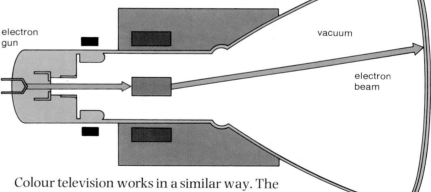

electron gun

vacuum

electron beam

This diagram shows how the image is received in a black-and-white TV tube. The electron beam scans the TV screen in the same way that the camera has scanned the scene. The screen is fluorescent. It lights up according to the amount of electrical charge beamed at it.

the three different signals are sorted out and fed to separate electron guns in the TV tube. These guns fire beams of electrons linked to the brightness of one of the three main colours.

By means of a special device called a 'shadow mask' or an aperture grill, the electrons which carry the blue part of the picture fall on phosphors which give out blue light. In the same way, the green parts of the picture are produced by the second beam hitting green phosphors. The red parts come from the third beam hitting red phosphors. In each spot on the colour television screen, the different amounts of the three main colours mix together to match the colours of the original picture.

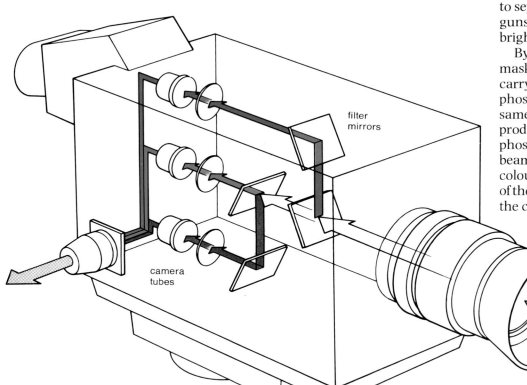

filter mirrors

camera tubes

In a colour TV camera there are three camera tubes. Colour, as well as light and shade, has to be converted into electrical signals. Light entering the camera is split by means of special mirrors into three separate streams of blue, green and red light. Each stream of light reaches its own target plate. The three tubes convert light into electrical signals as in a black-and-white camera.

The inside of a colour TV tube *(below)*, is coated with thousands of tiny dots of phosphors. These are chemicals which glow when they receive an electric charge. The dots are grouped close together in threes, one for each colour.

The pulses from the transmitting station enter the TV set through the aerial. They are fed to separate electron guns in the tube. These guns scan the back of the screen you see with electron beams.

The result is a continuously changing pattern of colour which matches the scene filmed by the camera.

In a colour TV receiver the shadow mask *(right)* is lined up between the electron guns and the screen. The electron beams are directed to the correct phosphors, red to red, blue to blue and green to green.

shadow mask

screen

colour coder

brightness coder

transmitting coder

decoders

30AX

A modern 'flat' TV tube designed to take up less space.

Video

UNTIL RECENTLY television was used only as a form of entertainment. However, it is now widely used in education, industry, medicine and to help in security. One of the reasons for this is that machines are now available for storing picture information on tape. At one time these machines were available only in the largest television studios. They were large and heavy and expensive. Nowadays, the **video tape recorder**, or VTR, is much smaller. It is also much cheaper to buy and is a common sight in many homes. The word video applies to any equipment which is used in the transmission or reception of television pictures.

Let us look at the problems of storing picture information on tape. You may know about sound or audio cassette recorders, used for recording music or sound waves on tape. Imagine a long piece of rope fixed at one end. If you hold the other end and shake it up and down, a wave is sent along the rope. The number of times the rope rises and falls every second is called the **frequency** of the wave. A frequency of one wave or ripple per second is called one hertz, written 1 Hz. The distance between the tops of any two neighbouring waves in the rope is the **wavelength**.

In an audio recorder, you have to record sounds with frequencies from a few hertz up to about 20 000 Hz, depending on the quality of recording needed. With video, the range of frequencies which you need to record depends on the number of lines in the picture, and the number of pictures per second. For a standard TV with 625 lines, and twenty-five pictures every second, the highest frequency required is about 5 000 000 Hz.

We need, therefore, to record very much higher frequencies on tape with the video recorder than we do with the audio recorder. This presents us with a problem. The picture information is to be recorded on to and read from the tape by a **video head**. We shall see later how this is done.

A video recorder in the home uses a cassette to hold the tape. It is called a **video cassette recorder**, or VCR. The video head is rotated at high speed, while the tape is moved sideways across it at only a few centimetres per second. However, the video head and tape must be kept in close contact if the picture information is to be properly recorded. The head is actually pushed so hard against the tape that the tape is distorted. This means that video tapes must be specially made so that they do not suffer any permanent damage.

Video tape is very thin and is made of extremely tough polyester film. This is coated with tiny, needle-shaped magnetic particles of iron oxide. These particles are 'glued' on to the tape with a very strong binding resin. This also contains a lubricant to make the tape run smoothly over the video head. When the tape is made, all the little iron oxide needles have to be aligned in the exact direction that the tape will

A video cassette recorder, (VCR).

The control desk of a prison security system. The system, in Jamioulx, Belgium, uses twenty-eight cameras. The television monitors show views from each camera for thirty seconds or so. If anything suspicious is noticed, the relevant picture can be switched to the lower monitor which has a video recording unit.

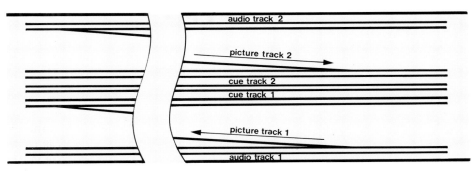

This diagram shows an enlarged section of the Video 2000 tape. Both sides of the cassette are recorded. The audio tracks are on the outer edges of the tape, the video (picture) tracks towards the centre. There is still space available for additional recording material in the middle cue tracks.

move across the video head; just like a long column of marching soldiers.

The VCR plugs into the back of your TV set to record programmes, or playback those on the tape. When recording, electronic circuits within the VCR change the picture information it receives from the TV into a varying electrical signal. The iron particles on the tape are magnetized as they pass over the video head so that they align themselves in directions which depend on the signal being recorded. After the tape has passed over the head, the iron particles remain aligned in their new positions. A magnetic record of the signal is now stored on the tape. When the tape is again passed over the video head on playback, the magnetic pattern on the tape is sensed by the head. This converts it back into a series of electrical signals which produce a picture on the TV screen.

There are three types of modern video recorder. They are known as BETAMAX, VHS (Video Home System) and VCC (Video Compact Cassette), depending on who makes them. All three use a magnetic tape 12.7 mm wide, but a cassette recorded on one type of machine cannot be played on the other. The BETAMAX and VHS machines use about 10.6 mm of the tape to record the video information. The more recent Philips/Grundig VCC system records the same information on only 4.85 mm of the tape's width. This means that twice as much information can be stored on the same length of tape, by turning the cassette over and using both halves of the tape. All three types of machine use the helical scan principle. This is the name given to the way in which tape is moved across the video head drum in a spiral fashion. The drum rotates twenty-five times every second.

This is also the number of pictures produced on the televison screen. The tape is moved sideways past the head drum at a speed of

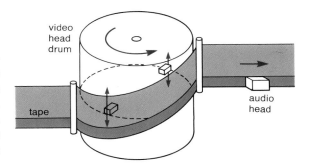

The helical scan principle. Tape is moved across the video head drum in a spiral fashion. The drum rotates twenty-five times every second. This is the same as the number of pictures produced on the television screen.

A video camera.

24.4 mm per second. A special electronic circuit makes sure that the head is precisely aligned with the track on the tape where the information is stored. This is called dynamic track following.

Video cassette recorders enable you to view one programme while recording another on a different channel. They have a built in digital clock so that it can switch on and record programmes even when you are not at home. You may also buy pre-recorded tapes of films, for example, to play at home when no programmes of interest to you are being transmitted. VCR manufacturers also supply portable colour cameras so that you can make your own films for TV.

Communication satellites

Long distance communications have improved greatly in the 150 years since Samuel Morse first used his electric telegraph. Today, messages are just as likely to be sent through space as along wires. Using a network of **satellites** orbiting high above the Earth's surface, messages may be sent across the world. Many of these satellites are operated by **Intelsat**, an international group of eighty different member countries.

The fact that satellites could be used for communication was first suggested by Arthur C. Clarke, the famous science writer, in October 1945. He believed that, one day, telephone calls and television pictures would be sent across the world, with the help of satellites. He predicted that if a satellite could be put into the correct orbit around the Earth, and at the right height, it would circle the globe at a speed exactly equal to the rate at which the Earth turns on its axis. This would happen if the satellite was put into an orbit at a height of 35 900 kilometres above the Earth's equator. It could be made to 'hover' above any point on the Equator.

A satellite in such an orbit is said to be **geostationary**. From its great height it can be used to relay telephone, telex and television signals from one continent to another. The satellite receives signals from one ground station, amplifies them, and then sends them back down to another ground station.

Telstar, launched in 1962, was not geostationary. It orbited the Earth in a couple of hours or less.

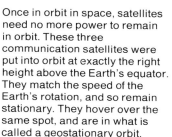

Once in orbit in space, satellites need no more power to remain in orbit. These three communication satellites were put into orbit at exactly the right height above the Earth's equator. They match the speed of the Earth's rotation, and so remain stationary. They hover over the same spot, and are in what is called a geostationary orbit.

The first communication satellites, such as Telstar, which was launched in July 1962, were not geostationary. Their orbits were only about 400 kilometres above the surface of the Earth, and one orbit round the Earth took only two hours or less. From any ground station they were above the horizon for less than half an hour. As a result, the large heavy aerials on the ground had to be movable, so that they could follow the satellite as it passed by. In April 1965, Early Bird was put into a geostationary orbit over the Atlantic Ocean. This enabled the world's first communications between continents (America and Europe) by a satellite in space, to take place. By January 1967, a second satellite had been put into orbit over the Pacific Ocean. In July 1969, world-wide communications came about with a third satellite over the Indian Ocean.

Since those early days, the speed, efficiency and cheapness with which signals may be sent across the world has improved greatly. Each day, millions of people use the telephone to speak to people on the other side of the world, just as easily as if they were living next door to each other. The world now has nearly five hundred million telephones which allow messages to be sent at the push of a button, or the twist of a dial.

The satellite Intelsat 1 (Early Bird) launched in 1965 could handle only 240 two-way telephone calls or one television channel. Some of the latest satellites can handle over 12 000 telephone conversations or forty to fifty television channels, as long as they are used correctly. Most satellites have to be renewed every seven years or so. In the future, this will probably be done by the Space Shuttle.

After communication satellites are put in an almost perfect geostationary orbit, they are not quite stationary as seen from a place on the Earth's surface. The aerials must point exactly at the satellite, and so some means of steering the aerial is needed. By homing in to this signal, the aerial follows the satellite and always points exactly at it. The aerials are bowl-shaped and range between 10 and 30 metres in diameter. Some are used to send signals (transmit) from the ground, and others are used to receive signals from the satellites.

The messages to be sent are changed into

Every day millions of people use the global network to speak to others all over the world. The messages are bounced off the satellites at the speed of light. There are ground stations for receiving and trans-mitting, similar to this one in Switzerland *(left)*.

varying electrical signals. These signals are then added on to a high frequency radio wave which can transmit them easily. It is called the **carrier wave**, and is of **microwave** frequency. This means that it rises and falls from 2000 million times to 14000 million times each second.

At the Earth station the signals on the carrier wave which make up the message are sorted out and fed to the receiver. This might be a telephone, a radio or a televison. The microwaves which carry the message travel at the speed of light (300000 kilometres per second). So, although a message from London to New York is thrown out into space and back again, a distance of about 75000 kilometres, it only takes about one quarter of a second.

International signs and symbols

BEFORE YOU LEARNT to talk you managed to communicate your needs and feelings through **gestures**, cries and gurgles. Babies use a language that everyone can understand. This kind of communication is called non-verbal (without words).

It is still very important after you have learnt to talk. When you are speaking, your tone of voice, the expression on your face, and the gestures you make with your hands underline the sense of your words. If you purposely make the wrong gestures the person who is listening may get the message that you mean the opposite of what you are saying.

You can use actions to express emotions that would be hard to describe in words: a kiss, for instance, or a shrug of your shoulders.

Most of our gestures are **instinctive** and are much the same all over the world. Smiling and laughter or frowns and screams are easy to understand as expressions of feeling. We all share more practical gestures too. All humans point, beckon and wave, nod or shake their heads for 'yes' and 'no', and count on their fingers.

Clothes can be expressive. A policeman's uniform, a doctor's white coat, and a judge's wig and gown stand for the jobs they do. All of us

People of all nations show their feelings with their faces, their arms and the way they move their bodies.

With their painted faces and special clothes, clowns are known to all the world. Most of their acting is by mime. Their language is one of gesture and facial expression. It is an international language and clowns seldom need to speak.

There are more than 5000 languages and dialects in the world. Even so, most people would be able to understand the meaning of at least some of these international signs and symbols. Some of them stand for ideas and beliefs and others are just warning or danger symbols. Certain colours are useful symbols, red means stop, green means go. Not shown here are the signals which manufacturing companies use to label and distinguish their products. Open a national newspaper or magazine and see how many of those signs you can find. All these signs and symbols take the place of language.

tend to choose clothes that show other people what we are like.

Pictures are international symbols. They often make a more powerful impression on us than words. Also, they are easier to remember. Advertisers prefer to use photographs of the product they are trying to sell than to describe it in words. Humans drew pictures of their surroundings, such as the cave paintings, long before alphabets and written languages had been invented.

We also need to attach pictures, or symbols, to our beliefs. The Christian cross, the Star of David, the circular symbol of the Campaign for Nuclear Disarmament, and the five linked rings of the Olympic Movement are examples of signs that stand for ideas shared by large groups of people all over the world.

Now that people travel so much between different countries, for work or holidays, pictures are used more often to give information in public places. You can probably understand all the directions, instructions and warnings shown on this page.

Most road signs are now international because they do not include written instructions (except for place names). In many of them simple pictures are used.

Colours can act as symbols. For example, red is a warning colour. Think of traffic lights, 'no entry' signs, and the red and white paint on a level crossing gate. A red cross on a white background is recognized everywhere as the symbol for the international medical service, known simply as the 'Red Cross'.

Numbers are international symbols. So are the mathematical signs used with them. These are really a kind of shorthand, but as all mathematicians use the same ones they are able to understand each other's work.

Like painting, music and dance can be understood by anyone, no matter what language they speak. Orchestras, bands and dance groups often travel to other countries to perform. It is quite possible for the groups to include performers from several different countries. Both musical notes and dance steps are written down using special codes.

We cannot do without words to communicate, but they act as barriers between people who speak different languages. Non-verbal signs and symbols are an important way of breaking down the barriers and in helping people to understand each other better. They are reminders that we all share the same world, and that we are all alike.

Languages of the world

ABOUT 3 000 LANGUAGES are spoken in the world today. There is no human community anywhere that has not worked out a language for itself. Each one is based on the life of the people who invented it, so it is specially useful to them. For instance, Eskimos use a large number of words for different kinds of snow. These would be of no use to people living in a hot country.

Language is a way of using symbols (words) in a particular order to give a message. We also use it to think and sort out ideas. It is very hard to think about anything without using words to describe it to yourself.

Languages change all the time. Words that are no longer needed in everyday conversation drop out of use, though they can still be found in books and dictionaries. This is often because the word has been replaced by another simpler one that most people prefer. For example, 'car' is now used instead of 'automobile'. Words can change their meanings, or have new ones added to them. Until quite recently, a 'computer' was a person who made calculations. Now it means a machine.

Hundreds of words are 'borrowed' from other languages. During the past, this has happened mainly when people invaded and then ruled another country. English includes many words that were originally French and were brought over by the Normans when they invaded in 1066. 'Court', 'saint', 'feast', 'beef' and 'vegetable' are a few examples.

Like many other animals, humans need to live together in groups. Sharing a language is a very important way of keeping the group together. Some small nations or groups of people are in danger of losing their languages. It is important to these people that they go on using their own language, and that their children learn it at school, so that their own culture is not lost.

Because language is so central to human life, differences in language can make a barrier between people that is hard to cross. It is difficult to make friends with other people if you cannot understand what they are saying. International organisations have been set up to try to cross the language barrier.

The United Nations Organisation meets in New York. Representatives from every country

in the world meet to talk about problems that affect all of us, and to try to help different governments understand each other better. So that they can understand everything that is said, each representative can listen through earphones to translations that are being made by **interpreters** while each speaker talks. The World Bank, the World Health Organisation and the European Economic Community are other examples of organisations that bridge the language barrier. Most of them use just a few 'official' languages. At least one of the five major languages, Chinese, English, French, Russian and Spanish, is understood by nearly everyone in the world.

Another way of solving the language problem might be to work out just one universal language. Until a few centuries ago Latin was used like this in Europe. All school lessons were in Latin and most books were written in it. People have often tried to invent a language that everyone could use.

A meeting of the United Nations Security Council. This council is responsible for keeping peace in the world. It has five permanent members, China, France, the Soviet Union, United Kingdom and USA. There are ten elected members from other countries of the world. Many languages are heard in the organization. The ones most used are Arabic, Chinese, English, French, Russian and Spanish.

This diagram shows just a few of the world's languages. A single language can vary and the variations are called dialects. There are about 5000 different languages and dialects spoken throughout the world today.

1	Chinese	7	Arabic
2	English	8	German
3	Hindi and Urdu	9	Bengali
4	Russian	10	Japanese
5	Spanish	11	French
6	Portuguese	12	Other languages

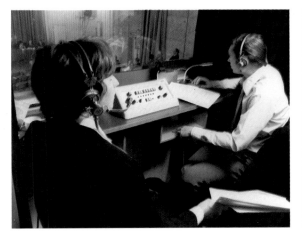

Interpreters at an international meeting providing a continuous translation.

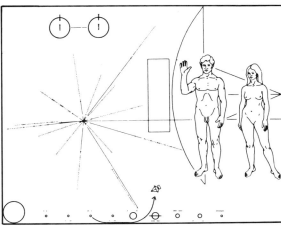

The Pioneer 10 plaque. Pioneer 10, which was launched in 1972, has now left our solar system on its way to outer space. It carries a special plaque as an attempt to communicate with other life forms in space. This shows a man and a woman alongside the spacecraft, as the creatures who built it. It also shows our solar system at the bottom. We may have to wait thousands of years for a reply, if one ever comes at all.

While we still have trouble communicating with each other on Earth, we are trying to make contact with other forms of life that might exist in the universe. The Pioneer and Voyager spacecraft that are now heading towards the nearest stars carry messages about Earth and about human beings. We send out many radio messages to other galaxies. If we were to receive such a message ourselves, would we be able to understand it? Scientists believe that the laws of nature are the same all over the universe. There is a chance that the scientific language that is understood all over our world could be recognized by other worlds, if we could only find them.

Summary

YOU HAVE NOW SEEN how we use language and communication in all its forms. Perhaps the most familiar is our use of radio, television, books and cinema as entertainment. This type of communication is meant to be pleasant and relaxing. Such feelings can be put over by using the language of colour and sound.

One of the main roles of communication is to spread knowledge and help people understand about the world around them. The basis of 'good communication' is the correct use of language. This is why learning about spelling and grammar is so important. Many jobs involve talking and working with other people. A scientist has to use very clear language to avoid confusion. A journalist needs to inform his or her readers of all the facts in a simple and interesting way. These and many other jobs need the ability to speak clearly and to use words and sentences that everyone can understand.

The greatest civilizations, from early times to the present-day, have had central meeting places where people come to discuss, or **debate**, a topic. For example, the senates of ancient Rome and Greece developed the art of verbal

Construction of the Tower of Babel, by Pieter Brueghel the Younger. Babylon was one of the centres of early civilization. The ancient city became the capital of a great empire around 1750 BC. It was famous for its hanging gardens and for the mounds and hills on which temples were built. According to the Bible story the Tower of Babel was never completed because of the confusion of many different languages amongst those building it. We still have this confusion of language, particularly in the great cities of the world. Any one of these great cities is sometimes described as a modern Babylon. You can hear the babble of sounds and languages as you walk in the streets of international cities like London, New York, Paris or Tokyo.

communication to perfection. The best speakers were those who always used all the facts to put forward their point of view in a clear manner. Such speakers were able to **persuade** others that their point of view was the correct one. If speakers use only a few selected facts, this communication may become what is called **propaganda**. This is when only certain parts of the story are given and a certain opinion is put forward.

Newspapers, radio and television are all forms of mass communication. It is now possible for a single person or opinion to be heard by millions of people. Newspapers were one of the earliest forms of mass communication but they are limited in their use because of language barriers. Television is a much more visual form of communication and so at times it is better at informing different groups of people speaking different languages. A flood disaster, say in India, can now be shown all over the world by satellite television without the need of words to describe the horror. This type of communication has a very powerful influence on our lives since many of our ideas and beliefs come from something we have read, heard or seen.

Some countries control their mass communication and allow the people to know only what the government would like them to know. This is called **censorship** and may be used for political reasons. Like the development of nuclear power which can be used for good or evil, modern mass communication can be used either way. Every time you hear or read about an opinion put forward by someone ask yourself if it is the full truth.

One of the greatest problems affecting world unity is that of language. Each country has its own language as a result of history and geography. For instance, a Japanese boy would be unlikely to understand a Spanish newspaper. One of the answers was thought to be the introduction of a **universal** second language. This was tried as long ago as 1887 when a language called **Esperanto** was invented. The intention was that all school children would be taught the same second language along with their own language. This would be one way of breaking down barriers between countries and of helping to promote understanding through communication. Unfortunately, this idea failed because of lack of interest by governments.

In the future it is possible that some of these language problems may be solved by **silicon-chip** technology. Already we have electronic **translators** which can change words of one language into those of another. Some modern computers are able to 'talk' to their operators in simple words. Perhaps one day a small machine will help us to chat with people all over the world.

Man is beginning to reach out into space in order to try to communicate with possible intelligent life-forms. For example, the Americans used a large radio-telescope at Green Bank in an attempt to gather messages from outer space. The results have not been encouraging, suggesting that we are alone in our part of space and must make the best of it.

Olympic stadium, Montreal 1976. The Olympic games take place every four years. Each time a host country becomes the centre for the games and pays for the organization. The games attract large crowds from all over the world. When we look at this picture we are seeing people from hundreds of nations and with hundreds of languages gathered together into one arena.

Glossary

acoustics: the science of sound.

amplifier: a device, as used in radios, that controls a power supply so that more power is given out than was put in.

amplitude: the distance between the middle and top (or bottom) of a wave.

amplitude modulation (AM): changing the *amplitude* of the *carrier wave* to match the signals being sent.

anode: a positive *electrode*.

anvil: a small bone in the middle part of the ear.

auditory nerve: the nerve which carries messages from the ear to the brain.

auditory passage: the tube connecting the ear entrance to the *ear drum*.

autonomic nervous system: the part of the nervous system that controls 'automatic' processes such as breathing and heartbeat.

axon: the long thin part of a nerve cell which carries an *impulse* away from the main part of the cell.

baffle: an object with a rough surface which will not bounce sound waves back as *echoes*.

band: a section of radio waves of similar *frequencies*.

base: the middle layer of a *transistor*, used to control the flow of *electrons*.

bilingual: speaking two languages equally well.

block: a piece of wood, metal or stone with a carved or engraved surface, used in printing, usually for illustrations.

brain stem: the lower part of the brain where it joins the spinal cord.

Broca's area: the speech centre of the brain.

capacitor: a device for storing electricity.

carrier wave: a high *frequency* radio wave used to carry messages as electric signals.

cassette: a small plastic box containing a *magnetic recording tape* which does not need to be removed for use.

cathode: a negative *electrode*.

cathode-ray tube (CRT): a tube which produces a stream of *electrons*. Where these hit a coated screen it glows to form a picture.

censorship: looking at papers, books, films etc, and taking out any information it is decided should not be read or seen by the general public.

central nervous system: the brain and spinal cord.

cerebellum: part of the brain, at the back, which controls our movements.

cerebrum: the largest part of the brain, at the front.

character: a symbol used in writing.

charge carrier: in a *semiconductor*, an *electron* is a carrier of negative charge and a *hole* is a carrier of positive charge.

chase: a metal frame into which type and *blocks* are fixed before being printed.

cochlea: a coiled tube in the inner ear where *vibrations* are changed into nerve *impulses* to the brain.

code: a set of signs used to send a message. It must be understood by both the sender and the receiver.

collector: the part of a *transistor* that collects *electrons* like the *anode* in a *triode valve*.

communicate: to pass information and ideas from one person to another.

compositor: a person who puts together words and sentences for printing.

conductor: a material in which an electric current can flow easily.

consonant: a sound made through a narrowed space somewhere along the *vocal tract* (eg, letters like B, D, S).

culture: a society's way of life, art and traditions.

cuneiform: wedge-shaped.

debate: to argue about a subject, usually in a formal, organised way.

decibel: a measure for comparing the loudness of sound.

demodulation: the opposite of *modulation*: taking the electrical signals forming the message away from the *carrier wave*.

diaphragm: in a *microphone*, a thin sheet of metal or plastic which vibrates when sound waves hit it.

diffraction: the way in which some waves, such as radio and sound waves, can bend around something in their way.

diode rectifier: a simple electric *valve* which converts an alternating current (flowing both ways) into a direct current (flowing in only one direction).

doping: adding an impurity to a *semiconductor* to increase either the number of free *electrons* or of *holes*.

eardrum: a thin sheet of tissue stretched across the end of the *auditory passage* which vibrates when sound waves hit it.

echo: a sound wave which has bounced back off a hard surface.

echolocation: a way of finding objects by sending out *ultrasounds* and listening for the *echo* from the object.

edition: the total number of copies of a book or newspaper printed at one time and all exactly alike.

effector: part of the body such as a muscle, which responds to a nerve impulse.

electrical resistance: see *resistance*.

electric current: the movement of free *electrons* through a *conductor*, such as a metal wire.

electrode: a *conductor* which leads an *electric current* in or out of a gas, liquid, or *vacuum*.

electromagnet: an iron bar surrounded by a coil of wire which behaves as a magnet when an *electric current* flows through the wire.

electromagnetic wave: a wave combining electric and magnetic forces, spreading out through space.

electron: a particle in an atom outside the nucleus, with a negative electric charge.

emitter: the part of a *transistor* that sends out *electrons*, like the *cathode* in a *triode valve*.

Esperanto: the name of an artificial language invented in 1887.

Eustachian tube: a passage connecting the middle ear with the back of the throat.

fibre: a single, thin strand or thread of material.

fibre optics: very fine glass *fibres*. Light is reflected down the inside of each fibre, and an image can be carried from one end to the other.

forme: all the type needed to print a sheet of paper, positioned and ready to print.

frequency: the number of complete *vibrations* per second in a wave.

frequency modulation (FM): changing the *frequency* of the *carrier wave* to send a message as electric signals.

fundamental: a note whose *frequency* divides to make higher notes called *harmonics*.

furniture: pieces of wood and metal used to lock type into place.

galley: a steel tray used in printing to hold lines of type.

geostationary: orbiting around the Earth at such a speed that a satellite always remains above the same place on the Earth's surface.

gesture: a movement of the body or part of the body used as a sign.

gourd: a fruit which becomes hard and hollow when it is dried.

graphite: a natural form of carbon, used in pencils and as a lubricant.

halftone: a picture printed in tiny dots, and made up of a range of tones from very dark to very light.

hammer: a small bone in the middle part of the ear.

hard palate: the roof of the mouth.

harmonic: a note whose *frequency* is exactly twice, or several times, that of another note, called a *fundamental*.

headphones: a pair of receivers worn over the ears to listen to a radio or tape recorder. They change electric currents into sounds.

Hertz (Hz): the unit in which *frequency* is measured.

Hertzian waves: radio waves.

hieroglyphic: a *pictograph* used in writing, usually Egyptian.

hole: a space left in an atom when an *electron* breaks free and moves away.

iconoscope: a type of television camera. The picture is focused on a material which sends out *electrons* when light falls on it.

impression: the marks left on paper by a raised surface of type when inked and printed.

impulse: a charge of energy which acts as a signal.

instinct: a type of behaviour that animals do not have to learn, but are born with.

insulator: a material that prevents the passage of electricity, heat or sound.

Intelsat: international *satellite* service.

integrated circuit: a complicated electrical circuit made up in a single piece of *silicon*.

interpreter: a person who translates what is said, so that two or more people who speak different languages can have a conversation.

ion: an atom or group of atoms carrying a positive or negative charge.

ionosphere: part of the Earth's atmosphere which contains many *ions*. It can reflect radio waves back to Earth.

language: a set of signs and symbols, with rules for using them, that can be used to *communicate* with other people, animals, or machines like computers.

larynx: the upper end of the wind pipe. It contains the *vocal cords* which are used to produce sound.

lead: an electric wire or cable.

lithography: a method of printing using a flat or curved printing surface. It is based on the fact that oil and water do not mix.

lobe: a natural, rounded division of an organ in the body, such as the brain.

loudspeaker: an instrument that changes electric signals into sounds, usually loud enough for several people to hear.

Mach number: a comparison between the speed of an object and the speed of sound in air.

magnetic recording tape: a thin plastic ribbon coated on one side with magnetic material. It is used to store signals that can be changed into pictures or sounds.

matrix (pl. matrices): a mould from which type is cast.

microphone: an instrument that changes sound into electric signals. It contains a thin disc that vibrates under pressure from sound waves.

microwave: a very high *frequency* radio wave.

modulation: adding electrical signals forming a message on to a radio wave which carries them.

molecule: the smallest particle of an element or compound that can exist by itself.

movable type: individual characters and signs on separate pieces of metal type which can be moved about.

moving-coil microphone: a *microphone* in which the *vibrations* of the *diaphragm* move a coil of wire near a small magnet, to make a changing electric current.

multiplexing: using one air channel or cable to carry many different radio waves or electrical signals at one time.

mute: a clip or plug used to soften the sound of a musical instrument.

neuron: a nerve cell.

nomad: one of a group of people who wander around with livestock in search of pasture.

n-type semiconductor: a *semiconductor* with a large number of free electrons, carrying a negative charge.

nucleus: the central part of an atom, containing nearly all its mass.

octave: a sequence of eight musical sounds. The highest has double the *frequency* of the lowest.

offset: a method of printing in which ink from a plate is transferred first to a cylinder then from there to the paper.

papyrus: a tall reedy plant used to make paper in ancient Egypt.

peripheral nervous system: the network of nerves not included in the *central nervous system*.

persuade: to convince someone, to win over.

pharynx: the upper throat, at the back of the mouth.

phase: the name for the different shapes of the part of the Moon that can be seen during each month.

pheromone: a chemical sent out by one animal that affects the way other animals behave.

phonetic: standing for the sound of spoken language.

phosphor: a chemical that glows. Used to coat the screen of a *cathode-ray tube*.

photogravure: the printing process in which the letters are sunk into metal and not raised as in letterpress.

photosensitive: affected by light.

pictograph: a simple picture used as a sign in writing.

pinna: the part of the ear you can see on the side of the head.

pitch: the highness or lowness of a sound, which depends on the *frequency* of the sound wave.

pixel: a very small piece of a picture, picked up one at a time in *scanning*.

platen: the flat surface used in some printing presses to press the paper on to the type.

p-n junction: the boundary between *p-* and *n-type semiconductors*.

prism: a solid shape with equal and parallel ends (often triangular) and sides with parallel edges.

proof: a trial printing used to check for mistakes and on which alterations can be made.

propaganda: information spread with the purpose of *persuading* people to believe in an idea.

p-type semiconductor: a *semiconductor* with a large number of *holes*, carrying a positive charge.

pulse: a regular beat, or burst of energy.

receiver: a device that picks up a message sent over a distance.

receptor: part of the nervous system used to pick up a *stimulus*.

recording head: an *electromagnet* used to change sound or pictures into signals on *magnetic tape*, and to change them back.

record playback head: see *recording head*.

reed: part of the mouthpiece of a wind instrument, which vibrates when the player blows through it.

reflect: to send back.

reflex action: an automatic response to a *stimulus*.

resistance: the way in which a material slows down an *electric current* flowing through it. Good *conductors* have low resistance.

resonator: a device, usually hollow, which picks up *vibrations* and makes them more powerful.

satellite: a small body in orbit around another body in space. Artificial satellites circling Earth *reflect* radio signals to other parts of the world.

scanning: covering a picture piece by piece in a regular order by an electronic device that then sends each piece out as an electric signal.

scribe: someone who is paid to write letters and documents for other people by hand.

semaphore: a type of *code* in which two arms are held in a different position for each letter of the alphabet.

semicircular canals: three tubes in the inner ear, filled with liquid, which sense movement and help the body to stay balanced.

semiconductor: a material in which only part of an electric current can flow.

sensor: a device that can sense an object, or energy such as sound or light waves.

silicon: a very common non-metal substance, which makes up a large part of many rocks and soils. It can be used as a *semiconductor*.

silicon chip: the general name for an *integrated circuit*.

slide: part of a trombone which slides up and down to change the length of the column of air inside.

soft palate: the soft area behind the roof of the mouth.

sonar: equipment for detecting objects under water by sending out sound waves and receiving an *echo*.

spinal cord: part of the central nervous system leading to the brain.

stimulus: a change either inside or outside an animal or plant picked up by *receptor* cells.

stirrup: a small bone in the middle ear.

stylus: a pointed stick used to write in soft wax or clay.

supersonic: faster than the speed of sound.

symbol: something that stands as a sign for another thing or idea.

synchronize: to keep in time.

teleprinter: an instrument with a keyboard used for sending and receiving printed messages by telegraph.

territory: an area adopted by an animal for living and feeding. The owner defends it against other animals.

timbre: the quality of a sound – the sort of sound.

transistor: the name given to a very small *valve* made of *semiconductor* material.

translator: a person or an electronic machine that changes the words of one foreign language into those of another.

transmitter: a device for sending messages over a distance.

triode: an electric *valve* with three *electrodes*. The current flow can be controlled, so that the triode can act as an *amplifier*.

tuned circuit: a device in a radio *receiver* that can be adjusted to receive an electric current at a particular *frequency*.

typeface: the design of a whole range of characters and signs used in printing.

ultrasound: a sound wave of a *frequency* too high for humans to hear.

ultraviolet: a ray with a *wavelength* just shorter than that of violet light. Ultraviolet rays cannot be seen.

universal: worldwide.

unpitched: not able to be tuned to a number of *pitches*.

UHF: ultra (very, very) high *frequency* radio waves.

vacuum: an empty space, with no air or any other matter in it.

valve: an instrument that controls the way a fluid (such as water or air), or an electric current, flows along a channel.

VHF: very high *frequency* radio waves.

vibration: a regular to and fro or shaking movement.

video cassette recorder (VCR): a machine that records television pictures and sound on a *magnetic recording tape* which is wound inside a plastic box.

video head: an *electromagnet* used to change pictures and sounds into signals on video tape, and to change them back.

video tape recorder (VTR): a machine that records television pictures and sounds on a *magnetic recording tape*.

vocal cords: folds in the muscles of the *larynx*. The voice is produced when the edges vibrate as air is pushed between them.

vocal tract: the passage from the *larynx* to the lips which produces the voice.

vowel: a sound made with the *vocal tract* open (eg, letters like A, O, U).

wavelength: in wave motion, the distance between the tops of one wave and the next.

Wernicke's area: a memory centre of the brain, where language is stored.

Index

64